Women and Men

Women and Men

A PHILOSOPHICAL CONVERSATION

by Françoise Giroud
and Bernard-Henri Lévy

Translated from the French by Richard Miller

Little, Brown and Company
BOSTON   NEW YORK   TORONTO   LONDON

First English Language Edition

First published in France as *Les Hommes et Les Femmes* by
Editions Olivier Orban.

Library of Congress Cataloging-in-Publication Data

Giroud, Françoise.
    [Hommes et les femmes. English]
    Women and men: a philosophical conversation / by Françoise Giroud
and Bernard-Henri Lévy; translated from the French by Richard
Miller. —1st English language ed.
        p.   cm.
    Includes index.
    ISBN 0-316-31474-9
    1. Love. 2. Man-woman relationships.   I. Lévy, Bernard-Henri.
II. Title.
BF575.L8G5713   1995
305.3 — dc20   94-33976
                10 9 8 7 6 5 4 3 2 1
                            MV-NY

*Published simultaneously in Canada
by Little, Brown & Company (Canada) Limited*

Printed in the United States of America

Contents

Authors' Note

This book is the result of some conversations that took place during a pleasant summer month beneath the welcome shade of a fig tree.

It has intentionally avoided mentioning current affairs and the world's distractions, from all of which we isolated ourselves for a few weeks to reflect together on the current state of relations between men and women. Thus it is, first and foremost, about love and love's byproducts — about desire, seduction, jealousy, infidelity, marriage, and about the end of love, falling out of love. Our opinions — and often our conversations — were lively ones. Each of us discovered in the other unsuspected traits and contours.

Our friendship, an old one, survived the test. We hope

that as they read us our readers will experience something of the pleasure it gave us to talk together bearing in mind those men and women who are no longer entirely sure what the verb "to love" means.

F. G.

B.-H. L.

Women and
Men

1

On Women's Liberation As a Subject of Derision

Françoise Giroud: Do you like women, Bernard?

Bernard-Henri Lévy: And you, Françoise: do you like men?

F.G.: I love them — their big feet, their little weaknesses . . .

B.-H.L.: And I like women for their high ideals and charming little ways.

F.G.: Fine. But seriously?

B.-H.L.: Seriously, I think that there's something very stupid about the way some men say: "I like women . . ."

F.G.: You do? I'm inclined to view that as the sign of being well balanced. Liking women is a rare thing for a man. They like to use them, which is something else.

B.-H.L.: What's unpleasant is the habit of regarding "women" as some amorphous group that's been put there for men to desire. I've always thought that professional "lovers" were not only ridiculous, but suspect. Having said that, it's true that I'm one of those men who — how shall I put it? — is aware of women.

F.G.: Well, I like them, even if they can be as hard and cold as stone, with hearts made of barbed wire. And I watch them, and as I do, I realize that in the past twenty years they've fought a revolution that is having a profound effect on their relations with men.

B.-H.L.: I watch them too. And as a matter of fact, I'm not all that convinced of the "depth" of their "revolution."

F.G.: Well, I'm no longer "operational," if I may employ that term. Nowadays my "experiences" are all on the level of friendship. But I see, I listen, I notice, and what I see is an amazing change. It's as though for perhaps the first time in history, perhaps since the days of the Egyptians, women had decided that they have a right to be happy. François Mauriac, who didn't like women much, once said, "Whatever happens, they're unhappy. It's their vocation." Well, I think that they've changed their vocation. And that has changed everything.

B.-H.L.: I didn't know that Mauriac quotation. It's a very good one, very fine. Terrible, but fine.

F.G.: More than anything else, it's frightening.

B.-H.L.: It sums up the whole history of literature, you know. The other day I was reading (one of the great advantages of summertime!) Balzac's novel *Le Lys dans la vallée*. Poor Henriette de Mortsauf, so in love with Félix but forced to conceal her love, to dream about it in secret — and then at last she confesses it, when it's too late, in a shattering and pitiful (that's the only word for it) letter. For her, desire is something horrible, guilt-ridden, somehow shameful.

F.G.: And nearly all she knows about it — which is the most incredible part of the story — comes from what she has read in books! In fact, she's ignorant. There's a "ban" on the very idea of happiness.

B.-H.L.: Yes. Although of course you'd have to be able to know what Henriette de Mortsauf *really* thinks.

F.G.: Oh, I think we know that pretty well.

B.-H.L.: And what if things were more complicated? More perverse? What if she derived a kind of pleasure — an unhealthy pleasure, but a pleasure nonetheless — from covering her tracks, from playing the victim?

F.G.: She isn't playing. She *is* a victim. It's been like that since the dawn of time. Read the Greeks, read Aristotle, Plato, and the rest — the female is seen as "evil," as a "threat" to the male.

B.-H.L.: It's the Pandora myth. Not only with the Greeks, but in modern times as well. You have the woman, often very beautiful, who spreads evil and disease throughout the suffering land.

F.G.: And there's another side to it. First, the man can never be sure of his paternity, which is enough to make him feel uneasy. So the woman must be shut up at home,

which was done. Next, it was thought that they would
sap a man's strength if they were allowed to.

B.-H.L.: Which is not, as it happens, all that untrue. Of
course, that's no reason to "shut them up" at home.
But it is true that women are formidable and intimidating creatures with a unique ability to play with
men, to dazzle them, to fascinate them — and, on occasion, to bring them to ruin. I'm rather fond of this
notion of women's inordinate power.

F.G.: And vice versa. But a man is never blamed for it.
Whereas the "man-eater" is an age-old image: the female with an insatiable sexual appetite who's draining
the vital energy of some unfortunate dope. That image
underlies all the imprecations that are directed against
women. So, "hold them down, restrain them."

B.-H.L.: There lies the fault. Because, I repeat, there's something attractive about the way men allow themselves
to be led astray, to lose their heads over women. All
the powerful men, all those conceited asses, all those
famous, influential men . . . Let a woman enter the picture and boom! — everything falls apart, the whole
carefully constructed edifice crumbles.

F.G.: As late as the nineteenth century husbands used to be
proud of the fact that they didn't arouse their wives
because they wanted them to remain amenable. That
was the result of the weight of twenty centuries of
Christian culture that had made female masochism
into a social value, that had taught women that self-

sacrifice was admirable, that suffering was more respectable than pleasure.

B.-H.L.: There, my dear Françoise, you're confusing two different things. On the one hand, you have the bourgeois mentality, the husband with his furtive, hesitant lovemaking, all of it a bit sordid, taking great care not to "arouse his spouse." You know Cocteau's famous quip, which I've always found very funny, and so accurate: "All husbands are unattractive." And, on the other hand, you have Christian culture — which decrees that there can be no pleasure without some kind of suffering, but which still has, we must agree, an appeal of another kind!

F.G.: Do you think so?

B.-H.L.: I do! Take the life of any female saint. Take any Christian woman who is in love, whether she's addicted to suffering or not. Sacrifice or no sacrifice, it certainly makes a change from someone like Ivana Trump! And it's much more exciting — much more exciting from the erotic point of view!

F.G.: I agree. But that's not the question. That kind of masochism, that enjoyment of one's suffering, that isn't a strictly female failing, even though we notice it more often in women than we do in men. It's been vastly exaggerated, implanted by cultural and social structures. "Suffering makes one nobler!"

B.-H.L.: "Cultural and social structures" have nothing to do with it. The link between pleasure and a certain kind of suffering, between sensual pleasure and a state of trance or self-mortification has existed for a long, long time, throughout the centuries — and, you'll pardon me, I don't find it totally without foundation. What about ecstasy? What is ecstasy if it isn't pain, if it isn't deprivation, painful self-annihilation?

F.G.: Forget ecstasy. For a long time, what Mauriac said was right. Women *did* like being unhappy. But now — I believe — the old structures have crumbled. Of course there are still some actual masochists, and in that case there's nothing to be done. For most women, it's as though a lead shell had melted away. They are just simply looking for happiness, and they're more capable than they used to be of fulfilling a simple and greedy desire for life.

B.-H.L.: What do you mean by "actual masochists"? I may shock you, but, admitting all the intolerable elements inherent in the age-old denial of a woman's right to love, her right to feel desire, pleasure, and so on, I personally am convinced that there is no female eroticism without at least a touch of masochism; and, vice versa, that a world in which they were all looking for your "simple desire" would be a much duller one. And for women themselves, too, of course.

F.G.: That's the male viewpoint if I ever heard it! A world in which women might possibly be happy would be a dull one! Dull for whom, I'd like to know? Even Freud, who was hardly, God knows, a feminist, never wrote that masochism was a component of female sensuality! I think that the past twenty centuries have left us more valuable things than "Christian shame," than the fixed and devastating notion of female guilt. Indeed, even though one may like it and charming as one may think it, the fact is that guilt is gradually being got rid of and that people are having to learn to live with women who are "dissolute" — I mean mentally. I'm not saying it's simple. But it's not simple for them either.

B.-H.L.: The question isn't knowing whether it's simple, but whether it's possible. You say "Christian shame." I prefer to call it sin. Or error; evil. And I think — you'll have to forgive me — that that sense of sin is something you cannot get around, something that's inextricably linked with desire and pleasure. That, since you've brought him up, was Freud's belief. And I really don't see how you can avoid this dark, or guilty, area of the sexual relationship.

F.G.: Who's avoiding it?

B.-H.L.: You are. Because you maintain that women's minds are being "rid" of a bad and negative way of thinking that has been created by Judeo-Christianity.

F.G.: Is it the "being got rid of" that bothers you?

B.-H.L.: Yes. Because it's rooted deep down in the soul. I'll tell you something: I don't believe I've ever met a woman — or man, for that matter — who was truly "liberated."

F.G.: I'll introduce you to some.

B.-H.L.: No. They don't exist.

F.G.: Well, you've changed the subject. I was talking about masochism, and it's my belief that for the great majority, it's an acquired characteristic, and one that's very difficult to get rid of. You come back with sin, crime, wrong, evil . . . very big words! Here, we agree: When it comes to things like that, neither women nor men are likely to be "liberated" in the foreseeable future. By the way, did you know that Chinese men and women have absolutely no sense of sin? And yet they have sex lives that are pretty intense and even, we're told, quite sophisticated.

B.-H.L.: And Eskimos don't experience jealousy. And they say that in the igloo the most hospitable act toward a stranger is to hand your wife over to him. It's amusing, probably pleasant. But I don't see what difference it makes.

F.G.: It makes a lot of difference to *them*. When they go to bed, the devil isn't lurking underneath.

B.-H.L.: Yes, but what difference to us?

F.G.: It means that somewhere there are human beings whose relationship with the act of love is different from ours. But that's another story. Let's admit the sin, the crime, the wrong or evil we can't get rid of. We still have to decide what's wrong or evil and what is sacred. I'm saying, and it's really quite simple, that women, through an immense effort, are in the process of liberating themselves from themselves. Who else does a person ever liberate himself from? And they're getting rid of at least a good part of the guilt that has for centuries been attached not only to their sexual comportment but to their behavior in general.

B.-H.L.: Well, what *I'm* saying — and it too is quite simple — is that you don't get rid of guilt "just like that." The human species is steeped in guilt. It is "originally" guilty. And so are women.

F.G.: Oh please! — you're not going to be so vulgar as to think that a woman who is liberated from herself is going to start running around like a dog in heat, the way men do.

B.-H.L.: Who's talking about running around like a dog?

F.G.: Women are rarely collectors, although there may be some. As a matter of fact, all the studies, to the extent we can trust them, show that — contrary to what people think — sexual mores have changed very little.

B.-H.L.: You see!

F.G.: But — and this is of major importance — language has been freed and, with it, women's attitude to their own sexuality, which they have become so bold as to want to be a happy, not an atrophied, sexuality. What a scandal!

B.-H.L.: I repeat: Who's mentioned "atrophied sexuality" or "collectors"? Who's talking about women acting like "dogs in heat"? If there is any animal behavior — and you're the one who's used the term — it has to do with desire in general, in the way it's been unleashed, in the games people play with it. Don't worry, it's under-

stood that here both men and women are in the same
boat. In the very same boat!

F.G.: It's all a question of merchandising. It's the mercantile
exploitation of sex in advertising, in music, in songs,
that has created this sometimes suffocating climate.
Unfortunately, AIDS may well serve to change things
drastically. When you're playing with death, you
don't play in the same way.

B.-H.L.: We'll get back to AIDS. At the moment, what bothers me is your "happy sexuality." Sexuality is never
"happy." It's never "innocent." It cannot — at least not
in my opinion — exist apart from a very ancient
world, one that exists in our very depths, which is the
world of forbidden things, a world of error, and therefore, inevitably, a world that is somehow bestial. I
don't see how that has anything to do with advertising or merchandising.

F.G.: I was trying to say that merchants are the ones who've
turned sex into a consumer product, into a spur to consumption. They can't sell you a brand of coffee without linking it to a naked woman writhing in ecstasy.

B.-H.L.: I'm all for naked women writhing in ecstasy! Including the ones who appear to be your "liberated"
ones.

F.G.: It's not only sex that's being glorified, it's — whether
intentionally or not — drugs, which are nothing but
objects of pleasure. "Unfettered pleasure," that 1968
ideal, has become almost an accepted thing.

B.-H.L.: Something with which, by the way, you go along. Basically, it's what you're saying your "liberated" women have achieved.

F.G.: Not at all! Our shackles are a part of us, they're an inextricable part of pleasure. But to go on to say that the flesh is never happy . . . I don't go along with you there, in spite of the melancholy that may be involved. And I do know women, many women, whose sexual experiences have always involved something bitter, something incomplete, because of an indifferent or clumsy male who has left them with their desire unsatisfied.

B.-H.L.: And I am here to tell you — to tell *them* — that I can introduce you to men who are more adept, or at least less indifferent.

F.G.: Go back and reread Stendhal, who was the first writer to cast a tender, unmisogynistic eye on women: "Some virtuous women have almost no notion of physical pleasure, so rarely have they been exposed to it, if one may use that term." I maintain, and I insist, that sexuality is a dimension of love that cannot — like death — be expressed in words, but that it is still an essential component of pleasure, of life.

B.-H.L.: Has anyone said otherwise?

F.G.: Anyone is free to seek happiness in abstinence, and I can conceive of that possibility. But you can't find happiness in some failed, castrated sexuality — that, no!

B.-H.L.: Obviously, we're talking at cross-purposes! You

know very well that I'm not preaching either castrated sexuality or abstinence! I'm saying — which is quite another thing — that all these stories of desire are still much more valid than we think, and that we're not all that far from what Stendhal was describing.

F.G.: No. Fortunately.

B.-H.L.: Yes, *un*fortunately. If you knew the number of women today who have "almost no notion of physical pleasure." Indeed, it's lucky for womanizers . . . it's what enables them to ply their trade. We'll get back to this. But if womanizers have a power, that's what it consists in: the ability to detect, beneath the mask of a supposedly "liberated" or "satisfied" woman, the face of an unloved woman, a woman who is usually just waiting to be recognized for what she is.

F.G.: Do you know Jean Baudrillard's piece on female sexuality? The history of femininity is in no way the history of some kind of servitude.

B.-H.L.: That's arguable.

F.G.: Far from being exploited, women, even in the depths of their sexual dissatisfaction, have always challenged the male's sexual pleasure, challenged it for being solely what it is, and no more. It's always been part of their strategy of seduction, and today they are supposed to be losing ground because they're laying claim to their right to pleasure, and so on.

B.-H.L.: It's not necessarily untrue. I too think that there's something challenging in a woman's apparent submission. And their power of seduction is — symbolically at least — equal to that imputed to men. It's what I was saying with regard to Balzac's Madam de Mortsauf.

F.G.: I needn't tell you that I don't go along with that argument and that, as a general rule, I find nothing more suspicious than a man who sets himself up as an expert on female sexuality. Including Freud with his famous "anatomy is destiny."

B.-H.L.: The advantage of Freud is that he has allowed us to get rid of all this talk about liberation — sexual or otherwise — once and for all. You'll forgive me, Françoise, but I can't get around that, and nothing that I've seen or heard, even today, can dissuade me from remaining a Freudian.

F.G.: A pretty strange reading of Freud!

B.-H.L.: People made a lot of this "liberation" in the sixties and seventies. They told us that everything was going to change, that everything was going to be different. They promised us a new day, a new dawn, a physical rebirth, an end to taboos, an end to prohibitions. They told us there would be a revolution, the greatest revolution ever. And then, when that didn't happen and we saw that the great change wasn't going to come about, they told us that at least the whole thing was going to effect an immense alteration in the way women thought and behaved, in their mental outlook. Well, I don't think it has. I never thought it would, and

today less than ever. If I had to say what I think is
going to last and what has changed, to pick out the essential, obscure, lasting element in the way people
think that has changed, I would emphasize the first
without a moment's hesitation.

F.G.: "They" say a lot of silly things, but you should never
believe what "they" say.

B.-H.L.: Of course. But "they" stood for a historical movement that mobilized people, that raised hopes, and
that, in my opinion, basically failed. Can we do this
book, can *you* do it, without bringing up the question
of what feminism started out to be, of the dreams it
created — and of its failures, the dead end it came to?

F.G.: A treatise on the joys and the trials and tribulations of
feminism — how boring!

B.-H.L.: You're telling me!

F.G.: In a word, I do not think that feminism has "failed."
Where the dreams are concerned, perhaps. But aside
from the fact that I've never been a dreamer, what
dreams *don't* fail to materialize? What would you say,
for example, about the dream of democracy? What I
do see is that women have shaken themselves out of
their torpor, that in a part of themselves they've become masterful, dynamic, joyful, humorous, whereas
women used to be sad, so dull. They want things — as
they say — and they're going to have them! Even if it's
become a movement whose goals sometimes seem a
bit foggy, even if American feminism got sidetracked
into a kind of frenzy of hatred.

B.-H.L.: You're speaking in the past tense. But it's coming back, that female hatred. It's what underlies today's *"political correctness."*

F.G.: What interests me isn't the future of feminism, it's the future of the couple, in society and in private.

B.-H.L.: Me too. That's why I'm so eager — on behalf of the couple, but on behalf of women too — to get rid of so-called feminist ideology.

F.G.: It's the relations between men and women and how those relations are affected, for better or worse, by the emergence of women who are imbued with a new awareness of themselves, women who can never be forced back into their former slots. What it's about, if you like, in the broadest sense, is power relations. I'm perfectly willing to agree that there are types of extravagant behavior and exhibitionism that are obscene, and that it's an abuse of the word "freedom" to use it in connection with that.

B.-H.L.: There's no need to agree with me. It's not at all what I was saying.

F.G.: It is.

B.-H.L.: No. I don't necessarily dislike exhibitionism. Nor what you call "extravagant behavior."

F.G.: Being free about your sexuality doesn't mean that you need to abandon your self-respect or that you have to wear your sexuality on your sleeve. What it does mean, to take only one example, but not the least important, is that sexuality has been separated from procreation. Do you know how many women have been mutilated for fear of "becoming" pregnant, as they used to say? And do you really think that nothing has changed in the history of men and women since that decision, the most important one of all, the decision whether or not to have a child, has passed into the woman's hands, since males have been, so to speak, deprived of it?

B.-H.L.: Now we're talking about something else.

F.G.: No. Because here what's affected is the very thing you've called "essential, obscure, lasting." It's been a revolution in the strict meaning of the term. And we haven't seen the last of it.

B.-H.L.: Listen. Of course I agree about what the separation of pleasure and the duty to procreate must have meant to women. But, aside from the fact that I'd agree even more if men hadn't been completely "deprived," as you say, there's still the other question, the one that the so-called feminist struggle has not answered, as you well know: namely, the question of what's happening in women's minds, what's happening with the way they envision their own bodies and the bodies of their partners, with their relationship to their own pleasure, their own desire?

F.G.: A *big* question!

B.-H.L.: Has any of that really changed? Has the revolution you're talking about affected, deeply, those areas of feeling?

F.G.: Of course.

B.-H.L.: Well then, that's our first real disagreement. You

say that there has been little change in "sexual mores," that what has changed is women's language, their approach to their own sexuality. But I think just the opposite is true: Morals have indeed evolved, there's been behavioral change, the attitudes, the strategies of lovemaking or seduction do not seem to be the same; but, on the other hand, the way women view all that has not changed at all. If you like, women are *behaving* differently. They act differently. But their inner thoughts and — I repeat — the way they view themselves and others have remained basically unchanged.

F.G.: Here, it's very hard to talk about women, in the plural. How am I supposed to know what all women's inner thoughts are? Who can? They've never talked about themselves . . . except rarely, or little. Everything we know about their feelings, their thoughts, their inner workings (to use a phrase I dislike), comes from what men have imputed to them. Men of genius, sometimes, but really . . . It's a man who tells us about Anna Karenina, about Mathilde de la Mole in *The Red and the Black*, about Emma Bovary. Later on, of course, we have Colette and her descriptions of what she called "the pleasures casually referred to as physical," but she's the only one.

B.-H.L.: Yes and no. Because there are some indications, after all. Little things. Without — and this is the problem — either the talent or the perceptivity of the books you mention. For that matter, some day we will have to face the question: How is it that the task, or privilege, of recounting female sexuality has fallen to men? Why this silence from women? This modesty? This abdication? Out of what prudence, what calculation, if you will, have they handed to others this obviously crucial task?

F.G.: Perversity, abdication . . . I don't see it like that. Where would they have spoken? To whom? Can you imagine a woman daring, before our century, to take up such a subject? Daring to do so even with herself? Daring to write about it? It would have been totally inconceivable. Where they themselves were concerned, they never, ever spoke of anything. Throughout history, women have been mute. And when it comes to sexuality . . . !

B.-H.L.: Let's take someone like Anaïs Nin. Of course, there's her *Diary*. But there's also that odd erotic novel I read a long time ago, it was called *The House of Incest*, or something like that.

F.G.: But there we're in the middle of the twentieth century.

B.-H.L.: Exactly! And reading it was like being in the middle of the nineteenth! Or take Colette Peignot, who was the mistress of three well-known men, the Russian exile and the French ex-Communist, Boris Suvarin and Jean Bernier, and finally Georges Bataille. Take that amazing woman, who inspired Bataille's *Madame Edwarda* before she died — quite young as a matter of fact — in his arms. A model liberated woman. A revolutionary par excellence. A modern woman who took part in all, absolutely all, of the struggles of her day. Well, *she* wrote a book. Or rather, after her death her famous *Les Ecrits de Laure* was published. And there you have a text, a very beautiful one, but one that relates female physical feelings in terms that barely differ from the old, traditional vocabulary. The enjoyment of suffering. Masochism. Pleasure in sacrifice. The likening of sexual pleasure to death. It's all there. All the stereotypes of what we call the Christian heritage. So we come back to the question: Does this evidence literary backwardness, the inability of words to capture a changing reality, the use of a masculine image repertory (in this case Bataille's) in the description of events, its description of her own sexuality — and all written by a supposedly liberated woman? Or does it demonstrate (and I am inclined to believe it does) the permanency of the great symbolic motifs that structure, that underlie, female discourse?

F.G.: Colette Peignot is an interesting character. Debauched, degraded, and beaten by one of her lovers, who made her wear a dog collar, fascinated by death, descending into the depths of hell in search of the light . . . In her case, we've gone way beyond the eroticism of suffering. Here we can compare her with Colette, who was hardly a sufferer. As for the moral value of suffering in Anaïs Nin, I don't see it. But let's get away from literature.

B.-H.L.: One should never get away from literature.

F.G.: We won't for long. For the moment, what I'm trying to

tell you is this: What has changed, exactly, is the way women have begun to represent themselves to themselves. This tremulous confidence they've gained in themselves . . .

B.-H.L.: That's why I brought up Anaïs Nin. What she writes is surprisingly conformist.

F.G.: So? Women have so little self-assurance, they're so ready to fall back on all the old tricks of seduction because that's something they know about, it's what they've always been good at, since time began. I don't see their being prepared to give them up, but they are setting out more and more frequently to assert themselves without relying on the shape of their mouth or their bosom. In short, they've begun to want it all, and that makes them ambiguous.

B.-H.L.: And attractive.

F.G.: Certainly. There are still some young women who are keeping to the old formula: Catch a man, as rich a man as possible, even if in exchange you have to put up with a few inevitable humiliations. However, I don't believe that that's still the goal of the majority of women, as it was for so long, although disguised in various ways. Even the most "dissolute" have their dreams . . . To run their own business, to go into acting, to write a book, whatever . . . To exist. "To express themselves," as they say nowadays. To assert themselves in a way other than through a man.

B.-H.L.: There's nothing new there either. You mentioned *Madame Bovary*. There's quite an amusing letter of

Flaubert's on what he also referred to as women's dual nature, their dreamy side and their calculating side, emotional but still keeping an eye out for the main chance. As he puts it, on the one hand there's the "cash register" and on the other the "dream cottage."

F.G.: True. But today it's the nature of the dream that's changed. Madame Bovary doesn't fantasize about setting up her own little business. For that matter, the women I'm talking about are certainly the ones who've changed the least. There is still a future for men who like that type of woman. As for women's approach to their sexuality, what has disappeared is resignation, patient resignation, their tolerance for a shared life situation that leaves them frustrated. Did you know that it's women, by a large majority, who seek divorces?

B.-H.L.: I do know one thing: it was at their insistence, and to their benefit, that divorce was reestablished here in France at the end of the nineteenth century with the Naquet Law. There's no question that in those days divorce was a female affair. There's a whole body of literature about it, a whole Belle Epoque literature that all deals with the same theme: the wife who leaves, slamming the door behind her.

F.G.: And finds herself on the streets because she's left with nothing.

B.-H.L.: Of course.

F.G.: Today, we've got statistics, and they're eloquent. Oh, such things never happen all at once . . . you have to give them time. But I'm convinced that a woman who is happy in her own skin won't decide to leave her companion. Women may sometimes find themselves alone . . . but they're much more particular than men. A man alone, widowed or deserted, can't wait until he finds another woman, and often it's just anybody. But women prefer solitude to "just anybody." For a woman to put up with a man, she has to have a minimum of regard for him. It's been my observation that that's not the case with men.

B.-H.L.: Has that happened to you, to prefer solitude?

F.G.: As a matter of fact, that unhappy choice has never presented itself. Let's say I've been lucky. But I *have* been alone. In my youth, I was very much alone, a lone wolf. Solitude is often very hard to put up with. It doesn't necessarily mean you can forgo a minimum of needs . . . or even a lot.

B.-H.L.: That's fine, but I'm not sure that it's the rule.

F.G.: Oh, it is!

B.-H.L.: You're going to tell me again that I'm not well connected and that you'll introduce me to some truly liberated women. But I'm struck by women's awful ability to put up with what can only be described as a kind of sexual distress. Of course, they don't admit it. It's a secret, their secret. They try to put up a front and they wouldn't admit for anything in the world that they are still, basically, Bovarys.

F.G.: That's a whole other thing.

B.-H.L.: No, it's the *same* thing. Because these are modern women. Dynamic, liberated, enlightened women, the women we were talking about a while ago, women who've achieved salvation. But as soon as you dig down a little, as soon as you get them to let you into their confidence, you hear such strange things, things that are very far from the happy, flattering picture you're painting. You find women who've been humiliated, women who are unhappy in love, women — young women, pretty women — who will tell you straight out that they go for weeks and sometimes months without even the hint of any show of affection. So they put up with it. Or they find themselves a lover. Or, as people used to say, they sublimate it and fantasize in secret. But what I'm getting at is that they accept it, they go along with it, and that here again, the female revolution hasn't changed much. Quite the contrary!

F.G.: Why "quite the contrary"?

B.-H.L.: Because they're fueled by something else. Isn't that what you're saying? That they've found different motives? Well, that — paradoxically — has helped to close their eyes to a lot of things, and, as a result, it's made them resigned.

F.G.: Now we've come to the real subject. Once again: Female resignation, in my opinion, is definitely on its way out. That doesn't mean, of course, that all women who are humiliated or unhappy in love will leave their companions. Not all of them. But enough of them will for a new female image to emerge, one that won't put up with a shared life if it entails injury.

B.-H.L.: So much the better. Yes, if you're right, so much the better. But frankly, I'm not convinced.

F.G.: And it's not only married women. There are all the women who break off affairs, to their companion's amazement, and leave, with their children under their arms. But that's something else again. Do you know what our conversation makes me think of? The words of my favorite Stendhal: "A man can say almost nothing sensible about what goes on in the heart of an affectionate woman." However, you'll probably come back at me with a similar statement with regard to what goes on in the heart of an affectionate man.

B.-H.L.: I don't know . . .

F.G.: And yet, I could venture to tell you, timidly, what is going on in the heads of affectionate young men, and there too, there's been a big change.

B.-H.L.: Oh?

F.G.: It used to be that for them to have a woman in their bed every night, which is what boys that age all want, they had to have a job. "Young man, you shall marry my daughter when you have found a job." And not only among the bourgeoisie. It was a real stimulus to work! Today, boys either do or don't have a girl in their bed every night, but it's got nothing to do with their having a job. The strongest motivation for young people to find work has disappeared.

B.-H.L.: What *is* true is that in these matters we hold opinions I hadn't imagined to be so different. I'm dumbfounded by your optimism, my pessimism annoys you. Which won't, in principle, be a bad thing for the rest of our conversation.

F.G.: My optimism? What makes you think I'm an optimist? Change isn't always synonymous with progress, and all progress has its dark side. However, something *is* happening. That's what I find intriguing and, in a way, moving. See you tomorrow.

2

On Ugliness As a Basic Injustice

B.-H.L.: Yesterday, after I'd left you, I reread Cesare Pavese's *Journal.* He says (I'm quoting from memory): "Women sometimes marry a man for his money but they usually take the precaution of falling in love with him beforehand." It's blunt, but it's pretty fair. Above all, it is a good illustration of what you were saying about those girls who are still engaged in trying to catch a man . . .

F.G.: You always love a man for *some* reason . . . why not for his money? After all, it's a sign of power, and women have nothing against power.

B.-H.L.: Is that your feeling? Do you love power?

F.G.: Well, not the power money brings! But I'm sensitive to intellectual power, certainly, especially when it's wielded by an attractive man. My weakness is that I've always loved handsome men.

B.-H.L.: The truth is that things cannot be considered in isolation. Do we love someone for this or that reason, do we know why we love them?

F.G.: Probably not.

B.-H.L.: It's like that character in Michel Butor's novel *La Modification*. It takes him the whole trip from Paris to Rome (and the entire novel!) to realize that what he loves about Cécile is the "face of Rome" and that "without Rome, away from Rome," he doesn't feel any desire for her at all.

F.G.: Result: his love vanishes. And at the end of the journey he's abandoned the idea of bringing Cécile to Paris.

B.-H.L.: Which proves that it's best not to ask oneself such questions.

F.G.: The truth . . . The sin of truth . . .

B.-H.L.: Which is what makes amorous situations so pathetic (and so charming). *Why* do I love her? And she, what does she see in me? Why this odd attraction? Through what misunderstanding? Lovers always ask each other the same questions, they always try to deduce, dissimulate, interpret. And, of course, they delude themselves.

F.G.: It's true that it's an endless exercise. Yet everyone engages in it.

B.-H.L.: And there are some girls who are desirable for a

hundred reasons but who spend their entire time wondering if people love them for their money. I used to know a few. I'd see them literally throw away their lives because they were always asking that question. Women who were stillborn, poisoned by suspicion.

F.G.: I've also known girls who were poisoned by suspicion. "Poor little rich girls"! But the difference is that a man can take pride in his money as a manifestation of his ability, his talent, whereas the rich young women you're talking about are most usually heiresses who've never really done anything and who think that no one could possibly love them for themselves. And, indeed, it often happens that they didn't receive any love, or an inadequate amount, in their gilded childhood.

B.-H.L.: You say: "My weakness is, I've always loved handsome men." Does that mean that for you attraction has always involved beauty, that an ugly man — I mean objectively ugly, unattractive, one who doesn't "conform" to generally held notions of handsomeness — doesn't or wouldn't have had a chance of attracting you?

F.G.: No chance at all.

B.-H.L.: You wouldn't have been able to love someone who looked like Raymond Aron, for example?

F.G.: No, I don't think so.

B.-H.L.: What about Jean-Paul Sartre? You were never attracted to Sartre, he didn't charm you?

F.G.: Attracted, charmed, yes. But I'd never have wanted him to touch me. And yet . . .

B.-H.L.: Please! Don't let me hear you say that intelligence can embellish or outshine ugliness. That's too easy. Be sincere and say, truly, whether Sartre's ugliness was an obstacle to you — and of what kind, of what nature — something that spoiled the attraction his conversation, his books, his fame, whatever, might have exerted.

F.G.: Yes. It was an insurmountable obstacle to any closer relationship. But I knew another frightfully ugly man who was nevertheless immensely attractive, and that was Pierre Lazareff. He wasn't turned down very often. Women dropped like flies. I adored him. But touching him . . . No: I can be friends with an unattractive man, but never his lover.

B.-H.L.: I'm not surprised to hear you say that about Lazareff. But the same was true of Sartre as well. He had lots of women around him, and often very pretty ones. But then, after all, it was Sartre, wasn't it, with his powerful personality, his strength? Do you remember what he once said? "If I became a philosopher, if I have so keenly sought this fame for which I'm still waiting, it's all been to seduce women, basically." And he didn't do too badly, in the end. But what if he hadn't been a philosopher, and famous? Isn't ugliness the insurmountable handicap? The ultimate injustice?

F.G.: No, I wouldn't say that. Handsome and stupid, that's no treat either, for a man *or* for a woman! And for a

great great many people ugliness is no obstacle to desire, in either a man or a woman.

B.-H.L.: That's true.

F.G.: What about you? Have you ever been in love with an
ugly woman?

B.-H.L.: "In love" — let's not exaggerate.

F.G.: Desired one?

B.-H.L.: Of course.

F.G.: How was that?

B.-H.L.: As all real lovers know, desire is a weird thing. You
can be moved by a voice, a form, a kind of smile,
sometimes a name, a family name, the curve of a back,
an image or phrase she's spoken, by some unexpected
vulgarity . . . or even one that's not unexpected. And
all that can add up — or come down to — a woman
who, by all the usual standards, might be regarded as
a monster.

F.G.: A monster! Good lord! I didn't mean to go that far!
Have you ever made love to a monster?

B.-H.L.: My case is of no interest. What I'm trying to say is
that if desire (or the unconscious) makes a choice, it
doesn't do so according to some imbecile logic. Beautiful women? Ugly women? There you have the whole
enigma of desire, its fetishism. You think you love a
woman, but you really love only a part of a woman,
one of her features, a detail, an inflection. And there's
the opposite, too, a reverse fetishism, which is the
woman who is truly desired, truly desirable, even lov-

able, but who suddenly ceases to be so because of some word, some gesture, some small detail, and so on . . .

F.G.: Yes, desire can be as fragile as it is sudden.

B.-H.L.: I remember a story that happened to a friend we'll call X. It happened fifteen or sixteen years ago. He was at his mistress's house on the tiny Channel Island of Chausey, just off the coast. A friend with whom he had shared a great many adventures came to visit, bringing with him another woman, older but very beautiful. X was greatly attracted to her. He even thought that, unfortunately, he preferred her to his own companion, the owner of the house. So they had dinner, looks were exchanged, various signals were given, secret understandings, veiled promises, ambiguous words. As the hours passed, his desire increased. Finally, to X's chagrin, it came time for bed, for each couple to go to their separate rooms. Now, after a while, after his mistress had fallen asleep, X had an irresistible urge to go to the other room to see if the "other woman" was prepared to carry through with her promises. The details aren't important, but anyhow he went, and when he opened the door he saw her standing completely naked against the fireplace while the other man, his friend, caressed her. The woman saw him and saw him hesitate (because of the nature of the situation, one last scruple with regard to his own mistress, who was, after all, their hostess), and then she

gestured to him to come closer — and while the other
man, who was pretending not to notice him, contin-
ued to service her, she said something, just one little
sentence, that sufficed not only to extinguish his desire
but to make it so that never again, on any of the occasions he was to see her, would he ever think of his desire with any nostalgia or regret. And what she said,
murmured, in what she probably intended to be a
very alluring tone of voice, was: "Come, come on, help
yourself!" You're going to say there's nothing so terrible
about that. But it was terrible for X. Because of its vulgarity, because of that hint of a "sales pitch," which
was so out of tune both with the intensity of his desire
and the quality of her marvelous body, and which
suddenly opened up for him a whole world he hadn't
suspected, the world that was her world. Just one sentence, a few words, and it was over. His desire had
disappeared. That's what I mean by reverse fetishism.

F.G.: Luckily she'd said it beforehand and not afterward.
    She spared X from having to blush about his behavior.

B.-H.L.: Why blush?

F.G.: Blush for having wanted to "help himself."

B.-H.L.: X never blushed. He might sometimes go pale . . .

F.G.: And for that matter, desire is never something to be
    ashamed of. You can't control it. It can't be evaluated
    in terms of good or bad.

B.-H.L.: I don't remember why I told the story.

F.G.: We were discussing ugliness.

B.-H.L.: Yes, that's it. The seductiveness of ugliness. The fluctuations of desire — and therefore, among other paradoxes, the startling way that ugly women are often very charming . . .

F.G.: Can we try to see how that works, how it functions?

B.-H.L.: Ah, it's complicated!

F.G.: Let's have a try!

B.-H.L.: Well, first, there's a touch of masochism: self-disgust, morbid self-regard, inverse narcissism and so on. There's a touch of sadism — telling a really unattractive woman, "You too have your charm, and I'm here to reveal it to you!" And then there's the urge to perform, to show off. Because, contrary to what people always suppose, it's much harder to seduce an ugly woman than a beautiful one.

F.G.: Really?

B.-H.L.: The beautiful woman is used to it. She's experienced and clever, she's been "run in," as they say. She knows both the tricks of seduction and the rituals of seduction. You always know very quickly whether it's going to happen or not. Whereas with the ugly woman . . . The ugly woman is so flustered, she's so surprised at what's happening to her, she begins by being suspicious, incredulous, by telling herself that there's something going on she doesn't understand, that someone's setting her up. And then afterward, when she has understood, when she realizes you're actually serious and that it's for real, she finds that she doesn't know the rules, she doesn't know the pass-words.

F.G.: Ugliness considered exciting because it adds to the dif-ficulty of seduction . . . I'd never thought of that.

B.-H.L.: And yet, my dear Françoise, it's elementary.

F.G.: Well, it's plausible at any rate. Quite plausible.

B.-H.L.: Not to mention all her so-called "complexes." Her body, with which she is all too familiar, her wide hips, her sagging breasts . . . All those afflictions that are her secret and that now she's going to have to reveal, to share . . . And does she desire you too? Is she dying to give in, to abandon her scruples? Desire isn't all that strong, it isn't so irresistible that she can forget them. That's why I say it's often more difficult to "persuade" an inexperienced woman than it is a woman who fulfils all the standards of taste, who meets the qualifications.

F.G.: That's masculine behavior. The opposite doesn't hold true. It's harder to seduce a handsome man or — to be more precise — a man who's used to being pursued, than it is an unattractive man who's ignored by women. Those just melt.

B.-H.L.: "Masculine behavior" — I'm not sure . . .

F.G.: Yes, "masculine behavior."

B.-H.L.: If I were to take an example, I'd turn to those eigh-teenth-century libertines who were always searching for the most dangerous, most risky adventure and al-ways decided that it was to seduce a flirt, what they used to call a coquette.

F.G.: Yes, they used to say they were going to "set out to get a coquette." On the one hand, there were the "prudes" — careful, difficult women. On the other, you had the "coquettes," women who were apparently easier. But it was just the opposite, wasn't it? The hardest was getting the coquette.

B.-H.L.: There you have it. What we could say is that there aren't any coquettes left. The true libertine action today, the prime libertine adventure, would be to seduce an unattractive woman.

F.G.: Right.

B.-H.L.: But with one caveat. With X, for example, it was almost a moral imperative: You could never "hide" your ugly women. On the contrary, you had to display them, treat them like queens. X liked very beautiful women, but when on occasion he happened to take up with an ugly one, he always felt that the elegant thing was to play the game to the end.

F.G.: The story about helping yourself could have happened to a woman and would have thrown cold water over her in just the same way. But I think the game of seduction is very different. Women are seeking the assurance that if they want it to, it can happen. But they don't necessarily need to "carry home the prize." At least not always.

B.-H.L.: Nor do men.

F.G.: You remember Baudelaire: "*O toi que j'eusse aimée, ô toi qui le savais . . .* " ("Oh you whom I might have loved, oh you who knew it . . ."). A woman can let a man go, like a beautiful "might-have-been," but I find it hard to imagine a man playing the seduction game without a real desire to see it through to the end. Similarly, most women love to dance, to excite desire, but most men loathe it. Arousal without satisfaction exasperates them. Am I wrong?

B.-H.L.: It depends. I can see a man operating that way. Seduction for its own sake. Gratuitous. Entertaining games, games of desire, infinite mirrors . . . But we can come back to that. For the moment, while we're on the subject, I'd like to stick to the question of ugliness.

F.G.: We're not going to end up concluding that the world is just not fair, that God made both the panther and the rat, the rose and the weed, lilacs and weeds. You'll tell me that the weed is unaware of the contempt in which it's held. Ugly, truly ugly people, suffer because of their ugliness, and that's a shame . . . truly.

B.-H.L.: Not just a shame. And it's not just suffering. The question, rather, is in wondering whether ugliness is not on the way to becoming our society's major prohibition. That was Romain Gary's perpetual theme. He maintained that we were living in societies that were based, not on consumption, but on arousal, on provocation. And he added that of all the methods of arousal, ugliness was the most unacceptable.

F.G.: It's not on the level of desire that this inequality seems most cruel to me, because fortunately many ugly men and women are loved. As the proverb says, "Beauty is in the eyes of the beholder." It's on the social level, it's the ostracism that occurs when a person is looking for a job and "makes a bad appearance," for example; it's the cruelty of children who don't like ugly people; it's the torture that women, and nowadays many men too, inflict on themselves to lose weight because society is intolerant of obesity, whereas others are able to stuff themselves with chocolates.

B.-H.L.: That's the level of desire as well. Because I'm sure you know as well as I that everything comes down to desire. Men and women can deny it all they like, but in reality that's all they think about!

F.G.: Of course. But what is a person with white, even teeth, with a lithe body, clear skin and glossy hair, all of which are demanded by our canons of beauty — what is that person saying? They're saying that they take very good care of themselves, that they're disciplined, that they know how to make the best of themselves, that they don't intend to let themselves go. It's a very significant discourse, one that goes far beyond actual beauty — which, as a matter of fact, is very rare.

B.-H.L.: I said *major* prohibition. By that, I mean that we're living in a time that is setting ugliness up as one of its fundamental taboos. It used to be sex, but that's been over with for years. Death — that's fading too. Very recently, Hervé Guibert even made a film in which he recorded his own final moments. So now we have ugliness, the spectacle of ugliness, this image of an ugly body — and that, I repeat, is something that a society centered on "show business" can no longer tolerate seeing depicted.

F.G.: You're forgetting that in the Middle Ages ugly persons were believed to be the devil's spawn. We haven't invented anything new.

B.-H.L.: All right, let's look around us, let's examine the language and discourse employed by advertising people, by salesmen. I'm not just talking about white teeth, tanned bodies, the dictatorship of beauty, health, and so on (although a lot could be said about this new "hygienics"). But — and this is much more disturbing — here we are, living in societies in which anything can be said, anything can be shown, in which nearly everything is either business or show business — and in which there is only one restriction, and that restriction is ugliness.

F.G.: Things are a little more complicated than that. There are many unattractive people on television, for example, which is our real window on the world. I don't want to hurt anyone by naming names, but no one would say that *all* of our newscasters, for example, are Greek gods! They can get away with anything — obesity, wrinkles, baldness . . . at least where the men are concerned. And in commercials too, you see all kinds of men. It's completely different when it comes to women — there's where the taboo enters in. A woman *must be beautiful* or, at the very least, pleasant to look at. There's an excellent female newscaster on Channel One whose voice is often heard but who's almost never on camera because she's plump, too fat.

B.-H.L.: We're all accomplices in that ostracism. You yourself—

F.G.: Yes, I'll admit that I'd rather see attractive, well-coiffed women. The taboo on ugliness is very powerful, and as for the one on age . . . But it seems to me that television tends to attenuate the taboo's harshness. Charming as female journalists are, and there is a growing number of them, they're hardly pin-up girls, they're not coiffed, sprayed, carefully made up when they're on the job, often in fairly difficult conditions. Their appearance doesn't always accord with some ideal model to be followed, and that's a good thing. It's a step in the right direction.

B.-H.L.: In May 1968 — or perhaps after, I don't remember— there was a newspaper that took as its motto "Free the Ugly." Stupid, of course. Totally terrorist. What they were trying to say was that ugliness was a bourgeois notion linked to a capitalist ideology and that it was therefore a matter of the highest priority that it be stamped out. How? By purposely beginning to desire what was ugly — yes, I mean that people were supposed to make up their minds, methodically, to desire ugly men or women. The idea was that for any true, militant revolutionary this was an imperative just as absolute as the fight against the tyranny of the assembly line. The whole thing was silly. But in its silliness there was an insight that wasn't quite so ridiculous, namely, that this question of ugliness sets up a separation, a division, that is, unfortunately, a decisive one, and one that is far more important than people think.

F.G.: What you're talking about is the revolt against the hypothetical notion that once all social inequities are removed human beings will somehow be fundamentally equal. But, I repeat, that kind of thing is in the hands of God, and, to quote Stendhal again, "God's only excuse is that he doesn't exist."

B.-H.L.: It's like Mirabeau, the great Revolutionary figure, who was so horribly disfigured by smallpox and who cursed Heaven — or whatever took its place — for having allowed him to become so ugly, so unpleasant to look at, so monstrous, and for having at the same time given him a soul — and not only a tender soul, but a susceptible, affectionate one. "I curse God," he shouted, "for having put the soul of an Alcibiades into the rotting body of a Philoctetes." He knew utter despair, unparalleled humiliation. "I have all the feelings, passions, desires, virtues of a handsome man and with them, this horrible body." There must be similar things in Stendhal, aren't there?

F.G.: Yes, on occasion he says that he doesn't like himself, that he finds himself ugly, but he's not as violent about it. Mirabeau, who had had smallpox in early childhood, seems to have been truly repulsive, but he was an exception. However, you know, no one — or almost no one — is satisfied with his or her appearance. Even the most beautiful women are keenly aware of their imperfections, they have convinced themselves that the whole world has its eyes glued to some minor flaw, some defect that they themselves regard as enormous. That's with the exception of a few highly narcissistic women who are literally crazy about the way they look. In general, people don't feel comfortable with themselves, which is why they have such a great need to be reassured, to be seduced.

B.-H.L.: What about you? Do you like yourself?

F.G.: No. I hate seeing myself grow old, but that's normal. It's ugly. But a few years ago I went through a very good analysis, and I came out of it with the ability, the art, to live my life with a certain amount of self-understanding. Insofar as that is possible.

B.-H.L.: In my first novel I invented an apprentice Lothario whose great ambition, quite naturally, was sexual conquest. His idea was that in the strategic war that any conquest entails, in the pincer movement you always have to engage in — which basically consists in keeping your quarry off balance — the first thing you must do is to discover your opponent's flaw, her one tiny, charming imperfection — which is also, of course, the vital chink in her armor. Once you've found that, the battle is half won. And there will always be some defect, he thinks, given the boundless nature of female narcissism.

F.G.: It is indeed widespread, but to very different degrees. Some women are capable of spending hours gazing at themselves in the mirror, caring for themselves, polishing and perfuming themselves, doing their hair, tanning, trying on one dress after the other for hours and hours . . . to mention only the most innocuous manifestations of narcissism. But men aren't exempt from it either, even if with them it's less spectacular, less associated with the body. However, I'm still struck by how many men today fear growing old, just like women.

B.-H.L.: Do you think so? I can't wait to grow old.

F.G.: I do. Even if it surfaces a little later . . . let's say after fifty. They really care about keeping that flat stomach!

B.-H.L.: I don't notice it. Indeed, it's my impression that the question of age is one of the basic inequalities between men and women.

F.G.: If you're trying to say that a woman of a certain age is always older than a man of the same age, yes, I agree. But, contrary to common thinking, I'm convinced that women put up with growing old somewhat better than men do.

B.-H.L.: Putting up with it is one thing. But the way other people view them is something else again. And for women who are aging, that regard is terrible.

F.G.: When you're growing old, you're busy enough with your own regard. Coco Chanel said something quite scary one day when someone expressed surprise at seeing her, so famous, so rich, growing old without a man around: "An old man, how horrid that would be! And a young one, what a shame!"

B.-H.L.: So, to conclude this talk of beauty, ugliness, and so on, there's one thing we have to keep in mind: the ability people have of taming, domesticating, subduing their faces or their bodies. It can be summed up in the well-known saying: "After forty, a man (or a woman) is responsible for the face he or she has."

F.G.: I think Degas said it, and what he said was: "After forty, one has the face one deserves."

B.-H.L.: It doesn't matter who said it. The idea is that one gets along with one's face; in the process, one creates it, even if only to disguise it. And there are few unattractive features that cannot be disguised, covered up. Isn't that the fortunate thing that seems to happen with so many women about whom people say, "Aha! She improved with time, she's grown more beautiful with age"?

F.G.: You can domesticate your body, but you can't domesticate your face, even by having a lift or having your nose bobbed. A face bears the reflection of our divine nature — and its opposite, of course, which in the beginning is veiled by youth and its attractiveness. But as soon as youth begins to go, everything written on the face starts to come to the surface and pretty soon it's permanently engraved there, and I don't know of any landscape that can equal a human face that's been

molded by its own inner character. No, you don't "domesticate" your face. You submit to it, you bear it.
And, if you have to, you bear *with* it.

B.-H.L.: Of course I'm not talking about face-lifts or things
like that. I'm talking about the game we play with the
part of ourselves — divine or otherwise — we call the
face. We bear it, true. Indeed, we forbear it. But we're
not doomed to do so, not inevitably. Indeed, there are
some faces that *don't* bear themselves, that don't go
with the body. Or, let's say, that don't seem to match
the voice.

F.G.: Faces that don't come together?

B.-H.L.: Something like that. Sometimes, in the same face,
there are elements — the arch of an eyebrow, the
smile, a look in the eyes, whatever — that seem to be
at war with each other. And in war, you have to resist.
People spend their lives, in a way, trying to bring these
various bits of themselves into harmony. You may fail,
I grant you that. It's probably also true that the people
who are the most determined to master their appearance are very often the very same ones who are most
outrageously betrayed by it — for example, those uncontrollable nervous tics from which André Malraux
suffered, a man who was a fanatic when it came to lu-
cidity and self-control. But at bottom, you still come
down to this: I would quote Levinas and say that one
of man's characteristics *also* resides in this bizarre
struggle to dominate, to conquer, to tame his own face.

With a little luck, he'll cease being this odious — or bizarre — creature. He will no longer be this excrescence, this rebellious object. And should I add that this in no way detracts from the obvious beauty of a face that has been molded by age and character?

F.G.: It's funny, but I don't feel that particular struggle, that inner disharmony with oneself, even if I do sometimes have the impression that I've "made" my face. But you're probably right, and the struggle is a part of the never-to-be-satisfied human search for harmony . . . with oneself and with others.

B.-H.L.: And I have to tell you that I wasn't aiming so high! Indeed, to speak frankly, I don't have anything against disharmony. Nor grimaces. Real ones. The ones Baudelaire called a challenge to the world. Until tomorrow?

3

On "Being in Love" As an Outmoded Expression

F.G.: Today, I feel like talking to you about love. Not desire, not sexuality, just plain love, being in love.

B.-H.L.: Oh? Do you think we're capable of making such fine distinctions?

F.G.: Distinguishing sexuality from emotions, yes. It's possible to be passionately in platonic love. How else would you categorize the Portuguese Nun or the heroine of Madame de Lafayette's novel, the Princesse de Clèves?

B.-H.L.: Well, there's certainly no "sex" in *La Princesse de Clèves*. No explicit sex, at any rate. But isn't it present in another way? Aren't there other ways of expressing it? For example, isn't the novel's heroine actually dying of love for Nemours, of her purely physical desire? It's as though we were to say that the great mystics were nothing but pure soul, that they knew nothing of torments of the flesh. Or that Bernini's sculptural depictions of ecstasy weren't replete with eroticism. To each his own religion, as they say. I, for one, do not believe in "platonic" love.

F.G.: I won't quibble with you about that. Of course everything is erotic, even mysticism. But there's still something we call emotion, isn't there, something in which sex isn't the only element — something, that is, that may not exist between people who just enjoy screwing . . . Forgive my language, but you force me into it. That's the emotion I want to discuss.

B.-H.L.: It's an old debate. For example, it's the debate that went on between the Surrealists and Georges Bataille — and, in a way, they said all there was to be said about it. The Surrealists believed in your platonic love. They believed in it because they were "idealists." And to be an idealist means to postulate autonomous emotions or feelings that were supposed to have a special, private sphere in which they held sway, a sphere in which they existed quite apart from carnal passion. And Bataille's answer was: "Oh no, such autonomy doesn't exist; there is no 'elevated' soul floating somewhere above the flesh," or, more precisely, the soul does strive upward, it continually lifts its head toward heaven, toward the sun, but its feet (actually, Bataille says its "big toe" — indeed, the text is entitled "*Le Gros Orteil*") are irretrievably mired here below, in dejection, in utter filth. And he ends by saying that that's why, because he believes that man vacillates between the ideal and filth, that's why he is totally incapable of imagining any emotion that might rise above, surmount, the filth, why their fondness for the wonderful, for Emotion with a capital *E*, their platonic love, seemed ridiculous to him. I'm not a great fan of Bataille . . . nor of the sordid side of love, for that matter. Nevertheless, I think that in this case he was right.

F.G.: Couldn't we just say more simply that human beings are capable of sublimating their desires, their urges? Which the mystics, for example, do. You can call that "idealizing" if you like, but that's the wrong term and it muddies the debate. In platonic love, what you have is a sublimation of the sexual urge. And I firmly believe that that can exist — less and less often today, probably because of the obsessive presence of sex.

B.-H.L.: Well, I firmly believe that such platonic love is a joke. Love is *never* platonic. You *cannot* love a woman without desiring — violently — her body.

F.G.: I believe in the power of "pure" emotions, in their ability to bring us to ecstasy, to despair, to all sorts of intermediate states. In short — and you'll have to excuse me —I believe in love. I believe in its reality, I believe in its poignant sweetness and in its awful violence.

The proof is that sometimes it ends and everything that once enchanted you in the other person becomes instead a source of exasperation. The bulb that gave off such a brilliant light turns into a piece of dirty glass; whereas desire remains. Oh yes, you'll have to excuse me, love does exist.

B.-H.L.: Don't excuse yourself. I believe in it too.

F.G.: Well, that's good news.

B.-H.L.: We're no longer talking about the same thing. Platonic love, no. Love per se, yes.

F.G.: What I find fascinating is that the emotion of love is no longer being expressed. We don't have any love songs, we don't write love letters or novels about love. Where is today's Werther? Who could dare write, without being called ridiculous, something like "She loves me, she loves me! My lips still burn with the sacred fire hers have kindled, ardent desires fill my heart . . ."

B.-H.L.: No one, thank God.

F.G.: You see! I'm not even sure people still dare say simple things — "sweet nothings" — to each other in private.

B.-H.L.: There, you may be going too far.

F.G.: Today it's as though the expression of true love were repressed, hidden, as though it were something obscene, the way people used to refuse to talk about sexuality. Barthes put it very well when he said that the obscene has somehow been transferred from the real of sex to the real of the emotions. All we talk about is sexuality. We calmly say that a man "has problems with his sexuality," but you'd bite your tongue before you'd say, "He's unhappy because his love isn't reciprocated." Our incredible physical immodesty is oddly matched by the modesty of our speech. What is the explanation for that phenomenon?

B.-H.L.: I repeat: Are you sure of what you're saying? I know that that was Barthes's idea, and it may have been true at the time, which was — and we mustn't forget it — more than fifteen years ago. It was the era of unbridled sex, sex of all kinds. It was a time when people used to say "everything is sex" in almost the same tone (and it may in the end have meant the same thing) as they once said, "Everything is politics." And it's true that Barthes's *A Lover's Discourse* was a welcome reaction to that climate. But now? Are we still at that stage? Haven't we moved into another era?

F.G.: In that connection, yes. The period of libidinal emancipation, as Lipovetski called it in *La Crépuscule du devoir*, ended when the right to unbridled sex received de facto recognition. Today, it's no longer old-fashioned to be a virgin, faithful, chaste. But nowadays it's more a kind of self-protection, a way of walling oneself off.

B.-H.L.: Self-protection or not, that's how it is.

F.G.: Yes. But at the same time, the porn market and things like phone sex and so on have never been more flourishing. Did you know that in Germany a fourth of the consumers of pornography are women? No, I really think that we've reached the minimal stage in amorous discourse. And the lack of love songs, which were the popular expression of a whole society — isn't that significant?

B.-H.L.: No, I don't think so.

F.G.: For example, who dares admit he's jealous? Jealousy is old-fashioned. Who would dare rhyme "June" and "moon" and "love" and "dove"? Love presumes a continuity of intent, it makes you think to yourself: Yes, this time it's forever! I don't believe that anyone still dares to speak the words that go with it, to come right out and say, "I love you."

B.-H.L.: We'll get back to jealousy. It's a whole subject to itself . . . as is this question of duration. For the moment, what bothers me is your notion of a society being eaten away by its obsession with sex and in which there's no longer a place for expressing words of love. It's very odd, but truly, I have exactly the opposite impression.

F.G.: And yet . . .

B.-H.L.: Of course there's this taboo on love, this verbal modesty, as you call it. But I think that we're starting to react against it and swing in the other direction. What was it you said, that the porn clientele in Germany was female? Good! What I *do* know is that where Paris is concerned, it has completely changed in comparison with twenty years ago. There used to be bars, there used to be specialized hotels, two-hour places whose addresses people used to pass around.

Whole areas of town were devoted solely to "pleasure." That's not entirely disappeared, of course, but
there's much less of it than there used to be. It's less
blatant, less vulgar. It's as though people had grown
prudent, very prudent — and, in the background,
there's been an amazing decrease in the ambient sexual potential, if I may put it that way, as well as a return to a kind of poetry.

F.G.: But that's not true!

B.-H.L.: Of course it is. For example, you mentioned songs.
Fine. It's true, I don't know a great deal about songs.
I'd be afraid of making myself ridiculous were I to
reply that love songs are coming back. So let's take literature — or, better, cheap literature. We won't mention any names here either, all right? But you know
what I'm talking about: all these contemporary imita-
tions of *La Princesse de Clèves* for illiterates, the so-
called romance novels. They reek of sentimentality.
You can find the words "I love you" on every page.
They're so saccharine they make your teeth ache. Saccharine . . . and more than a little mentally retarded.
Or take the cinema. Both of us have been involved
with the cinema, and in the same way. Don't you have
the impression that there too emotion, feelings, are
coming back stronger than ever — there's been a kind
of eclipse, yes, and now they're coming back?

F.G.: You don't have to know anything about songs. You
just have to turn on the radio. Wherever did you get
the idea that love songs are coming back? The other

day Julien Clerc was saying, "It's now a point of honor never to say 'I love you' in a song." And even cheap literature . . . There, indeed, sentimental stuff enjoys steady sales, so there's obviously a clientele for it, but what age are they? And they're exclusively female. As for the cinema, where's this year's great love film — or last year's, or any recent year's? And if there has been one, you'll find it was a costume film, set in the past. I don't say that love is absent from what's being written or filmed, I'm saying that it's no longer being verbalized, as though we were ashamed of it, as though it were a sign of weakness to feel strong feelings and express them or show them.

B.-H.L.: All right. Well, I say that the wheel has come round and that to me everything seems to indicate that our societies, bored with sex and recent plagues, are beginning to turn back to the sure, trusted values of emotion.

F.G.: I frankly don't see where there's been any return to the trusted values of emotion. Can you give me an example?

B.-H.L.: AIDS. I didn't want to acknowledge it, at first — all those investigations into the AIDS years, living with AIDS, new sexual behavior and so forth, really used to get on my nerves. But I am now beginning to think that it's marked a real turning point.

F.G.: Where AIDS is concerned, I think that there's something else, which tends to support what you're saying. Instead of the other person's being some pure and almost anonymous "consumer item" for the duration of the encounter, the consumer is now almost obliged to think about his partner: Who is he, where's he from, might he be contaminated? The object is becoming somehow a person once again. That's important. Yes, it is true, there is a change, a change that has its tragic side, but a change that is necessarily going to affect sexual behavior.

B.-H.L.: It's probably at the origin of the movement I was talking about, this return to the past. This new terror. This suspicion. The look of fear in the other person's eyes. The curse hanging over us. Bodies that are suspect, flesh that may be dubious — for some, it means solitude, for others it means paranoia. All those people who grew up with a taste for vice, with freedom as their religion — and who now feel that the trap is closing in on them. The "habits," let's say, that lovers are again developing — I guess nowadays we're calling them "precautions" — the return to careful lovemaking. As I said, I don't feel that it concerns me very much, but I hear what people around me are saying. And I'm obliged to recognize that there's been an enormous regression. Never in the history of mankind had we gone so far in the other direction. Never had we nourished so many dreams — illusions? — about total physical indulgence, fulfilling all the desires of the flesh. And never before has there been such a blow, such a crushing reprimand.

F.G.: Yes. From the birth of the pill to the birth of AIDS you had a kind of enchanted period. And it all came to an end with a cruel jolt. I feel concern because I have grandsons, and I fear for them. Drugs and AIDS, and one often leading to the other. I'm really afraid.

B.-H.L.: I have children too — who mean more to me than anything. But . . .

F.G.: Why did AIDS rear its head in the garden of freedom like some poisoned flower, like a plague created by Nature to decimate excessively fertile populations, or like fire from heaven to right the moral order, as some people have gone so far as to maintain? Perhaps there's no answer, but if you had to choose between them, I'd choose the former. After all, prior to AIDS, you had syphilis, which was perhaps less radical, but after all . . . It never persuaded men to put a brake on their desires.

B.-H.L.: Yes. "Less radical" it certainly was! And not perceived in the same way. It did combine sex and death, of course. And sin. And crime. Like AIDS, it made the slightest embrace a possible source of contamination, poison, murder. Except that of course you didn't die all that fast. And, above all, people never really thought that it would kill them. Look at Baudelaire and his correspondence with Poulet Malassis. He thought he'd be cured, right up to the very last moment. There wasn't that fatal, terribly fatal, element that AIDS has.

F.G.: And syphilis wasn't made into a media event, as we
     say today. People didn't talk about it, they tried to
     hide it. Yet think of the destruction, the horrible
     deaths. And the existence of syphilis, the terrible dan-
     ger of contamination, did not, so far as we know,
     change sexual "consumption" in the slightest, no more
     than ten thousand deaths a year from highway acci-
     dents keeps people from driving automobiles. Yet
     you're right, the fatal aspect of AIDS is spectacular.
     Will it lead to a real change in behavior, to some vast
     paralyzing terror, to anything more than a new market
     for condoms? You seem to think it will. For the mo-
     ment, what sexual consumers are feeling is anger, as
     though they were being deprived of some "right." But
     something about casual sexual relations is surely
     changing. Now there's fear. Perhaps it will bring on a
     new puritanism.

B.-H.L.: One thing is sure, and that is that we've finished
     with the notion — and the myth — of sexual inno-
     cence. A plague from heaven, you say, or natural
     plague? It's neither. On the contrary, it is a sign, or a
     reminder, of this basic fact: Love can be a thing of joy,
     sensuality can be happy, the union of two bodies can
     be a feast for the senses and for the mind; at the heart
     of every embrace, however, there's this touch of evil.
     It's what I was saying yesterday, if you remember, ex-
     actly what I was saying. And this is also what I had in
     mind when I emphasized the notion that there is
     something guilty about *all* love.

F.G.: But what's also certain, in my opinion, is that we haven't actually seen the first fruits of your new puritanism yet. As a matter of fact, there's really never been any puritanism in France — fortunately, let me say. However, it is true that among young people today we can observe what seems like a reaction to sexual promiscuity that involves disgust, a return perhaps to a new self-respect, a new discrimination when it comes to the emotions. That's the optimistic hypothesis. The other is that we're witnessing a — how shall I put it? — a collapse of desire . . . a collapse that includes not only purely sexual desire but all kinds of desire, a kind of widespread loss of appetite. It seems to me that at the moment, something like that is what's happening.

B.-H.L.: There! We agree. That's precisely what I was saying to you.

F.G.: It can happen.

B.-H.L.: But one thing more. You did say: "Never any puritanism in France . . ."

F.G.: I did say "never." Grant us that much, at least.

B.-H.L.: There, I cannot agree. Didn't we also have our "Victorian" era?

F.G.: Nothing comparable, not even in the darkest days of the nineteenth century. The French love life.

B.-H.L.: Here again, I think you're being very optimistic. MacMahon, the Moral Order, religious education, the Sacré Coeur syndrome — that whole era when, as —

F.G.: I'm talking about puritanism, nothing else. And I believe that puritanism is incompatible with the fond-

ness for physical, worldly things and sensations that is
an inseparable part of being French.

B.-H.L.: There, you must forgive me, you're just mouthing a
cliché. I don't see why "the French" should be thought
to have some special vocation for enjoying worldly
things.

F.G.: But their whole history demonstrates it.

B.-H.L.: Fine. Let's take it as given — we're not going to
spend an hour discussing it. You were asking me
about the romantic films of this year or of recent years.
My answer is: Almost all of them. From the film *Les
Amants du Pont-Neuf* to *Le Grand bleu*, from Luc Besson
and Jean-Claude Beinex to Rochant. Not to mention
the films of Eric Rohmer, which, as you know, are
about nothing else — although he comes at it from
quite a different angle. And as for the Americans —
when they make an erotic film they turn out something like *Basic Instinct*, which is a bad film, in the first
place, and in the second place causes a scandal.

F.G.: *Les Amants du Pont-Neuf*, which is the only real love
story among the ones you've mentioned, was a flop,
and *Basic Instinct* was a great success, including here
in France. And people flocked to see the film of Mar-
guerite Duras's *The Lover*, which is nothing but de-
signer pornography. But that's something else. I still
think that we have this kind of aphasia where the
emotions are concerned, this repression when it comes
to expressing them. And what I wonder is this: Is it

merely a question of language, or is it the emotion of love itself that's become anemic? Is it passion itself that's deteriorated? Is love now being experienced on a lower plane?

B.-H.L.: A film like Cyril Collard's *Les Nuits fauves* . . .

F.G.: There, indeed, you do have an expression of the emotion of love — it's even screamed at you, but in a rather special context, in the morbid, "hard" context of bisexuality.

B.-H.L.: It's a fine film.

F.G.: That's not the question.

B.-H.L.: As for *Basic Instinct*, I didn't say that the film was a flop, but that it had created a scandal. And that attests to a return of puritanism, not only in the States, but here as well. In other words, my belief . . . It's my belief that we're witnessing a withdrawal, an overall deeroticization — with, since we're talking about the cinema, all the predictable results.

F.G.: What do you mean?

B.-H.L.: The body, for example. Take the way the body is depicted. There are countless ways of depicting a body; you have the erotic way and the clinical way, you have the voluptuous body and the muscular body. There's the exciting body, the healthy body, the conditioned body, the one you know gets taken to the gym every morning and fed two jars of yogurt a day.

F.G.: The Jane Fonda syndrome. Don't forget to eat your fiber . . .

B.-H.L.: Right. And to an increasing degree that's where we are. And the linkage of that to sex, the omnipresence, the dictatorship of sex, has for some time now been nothing but an illusion, a pretence.

F.G.: I won't deny that.

B.-H.L.: You're saying that the emotion of love is ebbing. Or, more precisely, the expression of that emotion. And I'm saying that what's getting weaker is eroticism or, in any case, the intensity of eroticism. So maybe after all we're both right. Maybe the two phenomena are related, perhaps each of these decreases is promoting the other . . . Because the whole thing's connected. Desire, if I may put it this way, always needs two legs.

F.G.: There may be a reason for this verbal restraint, namely, the fact that people are living longer. I mean that the perception we used to have, our practical, concrete knowledge of the "life expectancy" of a love affair, a relationship, a marriage, has been altered by the increase in the divorce rate. As taken as we may be by the Other Person, as sure as we may be about our own feelings and those of the Other Person, somewhere in our minds, in our subconscious, we know that it's not "for life." In any event, we know that the people around us know it and that they're thinking: "How long is it going to last?" And when we're in love, especially for the first time, we find that repulsive.

B.-H.L.: Well, I don't think we know anything about it. We never do. It would be so much simpler if we did.

F.G.: Who gets married today without knowing, deep down, that divorce is an option? So we no longer think in "June-moon" terms. At the most, we reserve our options by talking about love in a low-key way, in that ironical way so typical of present-day conversations. We believe in nothing, so what would it look like if we appeared to believe in love!

B.-H.L.: A kind of world-weariness. Or early training in suspicion. Yes . . . I certainly don't see things that way. There could be another possibility though, namely, that we're on the threshold of some real mutation, some fundamental metamorphosis. After all, what we call "love" hasn't existed forever, not in the same forms. So from that to its disappearance, to moving on to something else, something truly different . . .

F.G.: Well, that would be a real mutation! Are you saying that love is no longer "the greatest concern in life" after having been that for — for what, more than three centuries?

B.-H.L.: "The greatest, or rather, the only concern . . ."

F.G.: Yes, Stendhal again.

B.-H.L.: I don't know. I'm tempted to say yes, love will remain the great concern. It will have been that for me. I am truly a member of a generation that, even when it was involved with literature, with politics, with whatever, even when it was engaged in the struggles or ambitions of its era, never lost sight of what Sartre said, that quote we mentioned earlier: Serious as the undertaking might have been, and as serious as we might have been about it, the guiding force was still the notion of seducing women. Is that still true of others? For the next generation? I tend to think it is. I don't have any real means of comparison, but I tend to think so.

F.G.: It was the case with my generation as well. In those days men were literally obsessed with women. Are they still, to the same extent? Probably, but the whole thing is more detached, plainer, in a way more honest. It seems to me that a lot of the sentimental trappings, to which women were greatly attached, have disappeared. Women today require fewer pretenses, fewer lies, plain desire doesn't have to be camouflaged. And perhaps they miss the civilized aspects of pretense.

B.-H.L.: I'm certain that women — most of them, at any rate — were indeed attached to all the rituals involved in seduction. As for men . . . As for men, I'm not so sure. We have two categories, the ones you were talking about the other day: There are men who like women, who really like them and who, were we to witness a general deflection from love and its codes, would truly feel nostalgia for them. Then there are the others, and for them, change would be fine. Bravo to anything that can "simplify" the process of seduction! Bravo for truth when it comes to the straightforward pick-up. Bravo for instant rapport, for openness, for the unlimited and unvarnished sexuality you see in those politicians who brag.

F.G.: Politicians — the poor things. Most of them have awful relationships with women because they use them mainly to heal the wounds caused by their failures. Are things not going well for me? Have I been defeated? Quick, get me a woman to tell me that I'm the handsomest and most intelligent of men, or at least to reassure me about the sexual vigor I'm about to exert for her. And any of the women with whom they're currently involved will do — and there's always one of them around. It's a hard job, politics, and you have to understand the men who engage in it.

B.-H.L.: The problem is that the women put up with it. And contrary to what you're saying, it's not necessarily just any woman. Not necessarily whichever one is available.

F.G.: I don't know which politician you have in mind. But, frankly, as a rule men in politics don't aim very high. They don't engage in real campaigns of seduction, they just don't have the time. They pick up whatever's available. And as we were saying at the beginning of our conversations, women love power, the exterior signs of power that always seem to attach themselves, willy-nilly, to a politician.

B.-H.L.: There's one exception, and that's our current incumbent, President Mitterrand. Without being especially devoted to him, I really think he's an exception. I don't know what he's like now, of course. But I remember conversations in the past with a man who

truly liked women, who was really interested in them.
Who still does today, for that matter . . . I won't reveal
any present secrets, especially since, obviously, I don't
know any, but I remember back, not so long ago, when
Philippe Sollers's novel, *Femmes*, came out — you remember, it was a novel with many characters that
were supposed to be based on real people, with many
real events. One day I was standing with him, Sollers,
at the corner of the Boulevard Saint-Germain and the
Rue des Saints-Pères; we had just had lunch and were
about to say good-bye. Along comes Mitterrand, with
Pelat and, I think, Roland Dumas. He stops and chats
for a moment. He reproaches me for not "coming to
see him." He realizes he's never actually met Sollers
before. We talk a little politics: the Communists, the
joint Socialist-Communist program. Sollers, who is in
great spirits, holds forth on the relationship between
the intellectual and power. Mitterrand says that that's
too important a subject to be settled there on the side-
walk, and so he suggests we come to lunch "one of
these days" to pursue it. The next day, the very next
day (and knowing Mitterrand, that's a record!), an in-
vitation arrives. A few days later (another record!)
comes the luncheon. And what do you think we found
ourselves talking about? The Communists, the joint
program, France, the world, the relationship between
writers and power, things like that? Not at all! Mitterrand had only one thing on his mind that day, only
one thing that interested him, and that was to know

who Kate, Louise, Deborah, Bernadette, the character referred to as Madam President — that one especially! — in other words, who all the female characters in Sollers's novel really were. He'd invited us just for that, it was the sole reason for the lunch. He wanted the "keys" to the book — which, by the way, he didn't get. The journalist Max Gallo, who was also there, couldn't believe his ears. He kept trying to get the conversation onto a more serious, or more elevated, plane. He tried politics, he tried "literature" in general, but it was a complete waste of time! And the lunch went on until late in the afternoon, but that day the President's mind (and what a mind!) was on one subject and one subject only, namely, *our* subject, the relationship between men and women.

F.G.: I'm quite sure he knows a bit about it. But I find it highly indiscreet for us all of a sudden to pry into his private life, whatever each of us knows about it.

B.-H.L.: Of course it is.

F.G.: Let's say, since it's certainly no secret to anyone, that he does indeed like women and that women, with politics, have been the greatest business of his life.

B.-H.L.: His particular case isn't important. What interests me is that there does exist a kind of relationship between a taste for love and a taste for politics, which is both fairly infrequent and rather likable.

F.G.: Oh, it's not that unusual — even though in his case he's an Olympic champion. But tell me . . . why do we speak so affectionately about a man who likes women and not in the same way about a woman who likes men? Why is the female form of "woman-chaser" or "ladies' man" so pejorative?

B.-H.L.: You remember that character of Huysmans who sets out to seduce a beautiful woman, brings her to his home, sets up a whole scenario, shows off, brags, the whole virile bag of tricks, and is suddenly taken aback when the woman takes over and gives a tiny, a very tiny, hint of taking the initiative? All at once she's damned. The devil in skirts . . . indeed, if I recall the story correctly, she later takes him with her to a séance. Well, that's a typical case. As soon as it seems that a woman "likes it," that she begins to take other than the submissive, passive role in lovemaking that some men want her to keep to, she becomes not only a "man-hunter" but a "slut."

F.G.: Huysmans was a little bit nuts. We might say that that attitude comes from the need to be the "master." I was talking about a special category, the female version of "woman-chaser," of "ladies' man." Such women are often charming, happy women because they spend so much time on themselves, and yet they have a terrible reputation. And it's a fact: they're looked down on.

B.-H.L.: Can we go back to something you were saying earlier? This evolution in the language of love, its debasement, and the notion — your notion — that if people are talking less about love it's because they've suddenly become wary of doing so. Life goes on, they know that they'll meet other women, other men; they know that the present adventure is probably not going to be their last, and so they don't want to make themselves ridiculous by indulging in the "June-moon" kind of talk.

F.G.: That's right.

B.-H.L.: Well, after thinking it over, I'm not so sure I agree.

F.G.: You don't?

B.-H.L.: No. Because I don't think that the fact of knowing, of being forewarned, knowledgeable, the fact of having chalked up some experience — one's own as well as other people's — has that great an influence on the mechanics of passion. Does the fact of "knowing," of having "data," keep racists from being racists, Communists from being Communist, anticlericals from being anticlerical? You'll say that those are odd comparisons, but they aren't, actually, because love too is excessive, a kind of madness or passion. And where passion is concerned, I don't think that "understanding," "logic," really come into play.

F.G.: The point is well taken. Logic never sheds any light on passion. So perhaps we should say, as you were suggesting a while ago, that love itself has begun to fade out of the picture while we are becoming somehow "de-civilized," that we're returning to the brutality of the kind of raw, savage desire that doesn't require words.

B.-H.L.: That's not what I was saying. Because "raw, savage desire" would be just fine.

F.G.: So what *are* you saying? That love itself can fade out

because it never really existed at all? After all, the
Song of Songs . . . that wasn't bad!

B.-H.L.: What's beautiful about the Song of Songs is that we
never know whether it's about human love or divine
love. The words are the same. The themes are the same
— today, we'd say that the fantasies were the same. So
that Eros and Agape, carnal love and divine love, are
both indexed on each other, totally interdependent.

F.G.: "My beloved is white and ruddy, the chiefest among
ten thousand./His head is as the most fine gold, his
locks are bushy and black as a raven . . ."

B.-H.L.: Yes. Well, perhaps that's what has disappeared, the
intertwining of the two orders, the two kinds of love
that nourish each other.

F.G.: And all we know now is the profane dimension of
love? Yes . . . It's a sign of our times that we no longer
know where to place the sacred. All that makes me a
bit sad. Until tomorrow.

B.-H.L.: Until tomorrow, Françoise. Because we've got on to
a very big question, and we won't solve it this evening.

4

On Jealousy As Consubstantial with Love

B.-H.L.: Sorry I'm a bit late. We'd started to talk about jealousy, and then we got on to something else.

F.G.: Right. What's your sign?

B.-H.L.: My astrological sign? Pooh . . . I totally refuse to take the slightest interest in my astrological sign.

F.G.: Being a Gemini precludes jealousy. That's what people who know about it say, at any rate. Lucky Geminis . . .

B.-H.L.: Fine. I must not be a Gemini.

F.G.: Well, let's be serious. Here is something that has changed: jealousy. Or at any rate, the manner in which people express it, experience it.

B.-H.L.: Oh? I'm not so sure. I guess I'm just not able to believe anything has really "changed" all that much.

F.G.: But it has. Once, jealousy was taken for granted. Feeling jealous was part of being in love, whether you were a man or a woman. Today, it's frowned on, it's old-fashioned, people are ashamed of it. But it does still exist.

B.-H.L.: Indeed it does.

F.G.: So that now you not only suffer from jealousy, but you also feel ashamed of it. You suffer because you suffer what you suffer.

B.-H.L.: La Rochefoucauld, with his usual exquisite irony, once said that jealousy was a disease, one that could bring on plague, madness, and mortification.

F.G.: So?

B.-H.L.: So, this downplaying of jealousy is nothing new. People have been jealous ever since people have fallen in love. And ever since there have been jealous people, their jealousy has been objectionable, unacceptable.

F.G.: People used to weep, fly into a rage, scream, fire off re-volvers, strangle their wives like Othello . . .

B.-H.L.: People still scream. They still fly into rages. And there are still men — even some philosophers, if you recall the recent Althusser scandal — who strangle their wives.

F.G.: There are almost no crimes of passion nowadays . . . that must mean something! Cruel, green-eyed jealousy hasn't changed, but it seems to me that today we man-age to dampen its most shocking manifestations.

B.-H.L.: It's odd, but I don't feel that things are that way at all.

F.G.: But they are! Nobody writes, like Heine did, "Oh my love, my love, why have you abandoned me?" We feel guilty about being jealous like we would about having bad breath. And men no longer weep. Have you noticed that men don't weep any more? That's something relatively recent. I don't know when it started, but in Goethe's day, they cried a great deal.

B.-H.L.: In Goethe's day, let me tell you, they cried at almost any opportunity: the death of a nightingale, a beautiful landscape, a battle lost or won, a glance, something they happened to see, a felicitous rhyme, a play — as well, in passing, at the treachery of a woman they loved. In other words, that doesn't prove a thing. Men cry less. That doesn't mean that they've become less jealous.

F.G.: No, not less jealous, certainly . . . nor have women become less jealous. That's not what I'm saying. Jealousy begins in early childhood, you know; it is first felt among brothers and sisters, and because you keep being told that "it's naughty to be jealous," you never really work it out, come to terms with it. I'm only saying that today we may suffer from it even more acutely because we suppress its manifestations. Have you ever been jealous? I mean truly jealous — not just the temporary irritation you feel when an attractive woman you happen to be with pays too much attention to the good conversationalist sitting next to her at some dinner party. I mean jealous with reason, or with what you believe to be a reason.

B.-H.L.: The thing about jealousy is that there are no reasons. Any one will do. There are no good or bad reasons, no real or fake jealousies, there's just jealousy — which will seize upon any sign, any indication, any proof or motive to support itself.

F.G.: Fine. But what about you? Have you ever been jealous?

B.-H.L.: I don't know that that's a very interesting question.

F.G.: But it is!

B.-H.L.: Let's say that I'm like everybody else. I hate jealousy. I know that it's an ugly emotion. But, if we're being frank, well yes, I've been — I am — jealous.

F.G.: Good.

B.-H.L.: But let me add that it's generally for what you would call frivolous or fictional reasons. Because it is as we were saying, isn't it: When it comes to this, there are no more-or-less valid reasons. Viewed from the outside, truly jealous people never seem to have a rational motive for being jealous. They just are, that's all, without any rhyme or reason. It's a disaster, a poison, and they become intoxicated by that poison.

F.G.: I'll tell you a story about jealousy. I was sixteen, I was in love with a thirty-year-old man, madly in love, I loved him in my very bones — and indeed, he was especially "lovable." I worked with him, he was fond of me, he liked being with me, he treated me like a little sister — perhaps with a touch of incest — he was always doing nice things for me. And then one evening, in my presence, he dialed a telephone number in

Berlin . . . I can still remember it vividly. He proceeded to have a conversation with a woman I knew, an actress, one of those endless, whispered conversations lovers have with each other at night. It took me a few minutes to understand what was going on. And then, furious, I picked up a vase and threw it to the floor, breaking it. He looked up at me, he said: "Oh, I'd forgotten you were here," and then he just went on talking. I felt so humiliated, such a burning sensation, such shame, that since then nobody, no one, has ever made me show jealousy. As a matter of fact, in all my life I've never made what people call a scene, for any reason.

B.-H.L.: Is that the barbed wire in the heart you were talking about the other day? It's so hard to "contain" jealousy. It is so much a part of love. It's so consubstantial with it.

F.G.: Yet there are natures that are jealous to greater or lesser degrees, more or less prompt to be suspicious.

B.-H.L.: Every woman is not Phaedre, fortunately.

F.G.: Nor all men Alcestis.

B.-H.L.: But jealousy is still jealousy.

F.G.: Some men can drive you crazy. I knew a pathologically jealous man who was also one of the world's wittiest. When he had a fit of jealousy he turned stupid and vulgar, truly vulgar, in his accusations, in what he imagined he'd noticed. For him, anything could be a pretext — a word, a smile, a frown, a new dress. He would have liked to keep me in a drawer and take me out to enjoy all by himself, and he even had the nerve to tell me so! But it's a proof of love, he used to say, a proof of love! I ended up getting rid of the whole thing, him and his proof. Because with jealousy, the tragedy is that the more you feel you're being watched, spied on, the more stifling it becomes and the more tempted you are to provide some reason for all the suspicion. It's a degrading process.

B.-H.L.: It depends. There are two ways in which the person subjected to it can confront jealousy. He can find it stifling, of course. But he can also take it (and from this standpoint "your" jealous man was not so wrong) as a proof— or in any event as a sign — that he's in love. There are some women who expect such a sign. Some even demand it. If you aren't jealous, or aren't jealous enough, they view it as an indication, an omen, that the affair is over. How many men have heard a woman they may indeed no longer love, or are beginning to love less, say to them, "You aren't even jealous anymore"? How many have played the jealous scene! To echo a famous quip: "What happened to the days when you used to be so morbidly jealous?"

F.G.: The total absence of any sign of jealousy is indeed disturbing, and it *can* be taken for the onset of indifference. But there are little signs . . . and then there are big ones. I'm all for the little signs. I'm less enthusiastic about the big ones.

B.-H.L.: Amen.

F.G.: That being said, the worst kind of jealousy is retrospective jealousy. That's real torture for both parties.
Nothing can appease it. It's not, "You don't love me
any more." It's "Who did you love *before* you loved
me?" It's horrible.

B.-H.L.: Yes, horrible. But at the same time — and it's a terrible thing to say — it's also love! As you know, Proust
says that jealousy is the essence of love. But then he
goes on to say that the essence of jealousy is retrospective jealousy. Why? Because love is possession, and
you do not really possess someone if all you have is
this ridiculous little piece of them, their present.
Proust is in love with Reynaldo Hahn. He desires him.
And because he desires him, truly desires him, he tries
to know everything, to control and if possible to anni-
hilate the part of Reynaldo that eludes him, the part of
him that is, by definition, his past. I'm not saying it's
funny, or that a person should not try at all costs to rid
oneself of that kind of jealousy. Indeed, that is something that Proust (as his *Correspondence* shows) regu-
larly vowed to do. But that's the way it is, and that's
probably how it has to be. Jealousy, unfortunately, is
part of the game.

F.G.: But no one ever possesses anyone else! It's a monstrous notion, a crazy one. The most you can claim is
what you've changed about them, the way they do
their hair, the color of their ties. You know nothing of
the other person, what he's like when he's out of sight.

And as for his past! As a matter of fact, they would probably be very boring, someone you could totally "possess," who would hold no surprises, have no shadows . . .

B.-H.L.: I don't know . . .

F.G.: Proust's heroes have strange partners who have pretty varied pasts. But they probably didn't pick them at random, and it's their very ambiguity, their oddness, their untouchableness, that makes them desirable. In the end, no one has ever written about jealousy better, and we should blush to talk about it after him.

B.-H.L.: Oh, blush . . . If we have to blush for that, along with everything else . . .

F.G.: *The Fugitive* is a masterpiece.

B.-H.L.: Indeed. For example, on the question of retrospective jealousy . . .

F.G.: Yes?

B.-H.L.: Here, I repeat, we agree. And those who don't control themselves, who do not suppress their jealousy, those who don't do everything they can to avoid showing it, who allow it to have a voice, to spread like a cancer, to propagate and seep into every cranny, into every shadowy part of the past — people like that, be they men or women, will obviously very quickly become unbearable. What makes *The Fugitive* such a magnificent novel is that in it Proust is speaking to us about the very essence of love, its ultimate temptations. And from that viewpoint (from the viewpoint of what is almost a "chemical" analysis of the phenomenon) his is a cruel and implacable description: Jealousy may well be a morbid, unhealthy, monstrous process, it may well be a cancer, the leukemia of the soul — but it is also, alas, a (essential) component of love.

F.G.: And, alas, I must agree with you. "Alas," because it causes pain, and more than pain. But I think that with a couple, there's always one who is more readily a prey to jealousy than the other, more a prey to self-torture, self-torment, more prepared to seize upon the slightest pretext. There must surely be a tendency to jealousy, something Proust must have possessed to a high degree. Swann is jealous, Odette isn't. Is it because she doesn't love him?

B.-H.L.: Of course.

F.G.: The Narrator of *Remembrance* is jealous, Albertine is not. The same reason?

B.-H.L.: Obviously.

F.G.: But it's not just a fluke if you fall in love with someone whose feelings for you are tepid, someone who only likes to *be* loved.

B.-H.L.: That's not what I'm saying. Because, at the same time, I do believe in the possibility of reciprocal love.

F.G.: You said "no happy love."

B.-H.L.: That doesn't rule out reciprocity. Even if it is based on misunderstanding. The *passionate* reciprocity of misunderstanding.

F.G.: There's a certain tendency — it's the only word that

comes to my mind — to fall unhappily in love. Especially since . . .

B.-H.L.: Deleuze was at one point struck by another of
Proust's ideas. I find it very apt! Jealousy, he says, is
hermeneutic, it's a science of interpretation, a science
of signs and their significance. One is never jealous of
a "fact," after all. One is never jealous — with the exception of scenes like the one you recounted — that
your partner will cheat on you, betray you, leave you.
He may very well cheat on you, let him! It will be
terrible, you'll suffer, you may cheat on him in return.
However . . .

F.G.: That's what you must never do. Bad therapy. It's the
surest way to suffer twice as much.

B.-H.L.: I agree. But let's keep ourselves out of it. What trig-
gers jealousy, what really sets it in motion, is things
that are far more tenuous, a look, for example, an expression on the face of the woman you love. A mood
you haven't seen before. A conversation that seems to
last too long. A suspicious interest. Even a caress . . .

F.G.: A caress?

B.-H.L.: Yes, one can be jealous of a caress. Oh, not someone
else's caress! No, a caress *you* receive, a marvelous caress, a delightful one, but one that you suddenly feel is
odd, not like the others. One that makes you wonder
where in the hell it comes from, in what depths she
discovered it. You can be jealous of a word, of a
slightly different tone of voice. One is jealous of tiny

things, and the tinier they are, the more intense the jealousy. Signs, yes: always signs. And around those signs there springs up a kind of interpretative mania, a science of decoding.

F.G.: That reminds me of a funny story about Helène Lazareff. She was very fond of men, as you know. She went to the United States with her husband, and when they came back I noticed that she'd taken to smoking French cigarettes. I deduced that a new lover — I won't mention his name — had come into her life, and I was right.

B.-H.L.: The question is, did her husband notice it too?

F.G.: I'm afraid so, unfortunately.

B.-H.L.: There you are. It's like that other, more recent, story. There was a man who was making every possible effort to conceal his double life, and managing quite well. He had taken all kinds of extraordinarily sophisticated precautions save one, which betrayed him: it was one word, a new word, that he happened to use. A little, simple, but completely incongruous, word, a word that wasn't like him. And that small lexical error brought the whole thing tumbling down.

F.G.: It's what makes the difference between the two kinds of jealous person. There's the one who avidly seizes on anything that can feed the beast within him, always on the alert, and there's the other, perhaps a bit dense, who is purposely less watchful, less eager to suffer.

B.-H.L.: I don't know if you can differentiate between them because I don't know how you can tell which is which. Recent literature has come up with two great examples of jealousy. Nathan, the hero of *Sophie's Choice*, and Solal, the hero of Albert Cohen's novel *Belle du Seigneur*, both of which contain shocking scenes of jealousy. Not to mention the character in Luis Bunuel's film *El*, who resembles them both. In which of your categories would you put them?

F.G.: I don't remember *Sophie's Choice* all that well. Solal is above all an actor, I find, a man with an ego as big as a house. He performs the great scene of jealousy just as he performed the great love scene. The very thought of his having had a predecessor in Ariane's bed — in her heart, rather — drives him crazy for reasons that are hardly "Proustian," but because it makes him feel somehow diminished. Of course, if his predecessor had been the king of Egypt he would take it differently, but just some run-of-the-mill orchestra conductor . . . He suffers, yes, and terribly, but it's really his vanity that suffers.

B.-H.L.: Are you sure of your "scenario"? Are you certain that his jealousy is based on vanity?

F.G.: That's how I interpret it.

B.-H.L.: I don't recall it like that. I recall a more irrational Solal, a man who is more truly tortured, and more crazed.

F.G.: He finds that he's loved by a completely ordinary

woman who on one occasion had a weakness for an ordinary man. He can't bear it.

B.-H.L.: Speaking of Albert Cohen — he's a writer little known to Anglo-Saxon readers, unfortunately, because he has never been translated into English, but who has a great reputation in France, a reputation based primarily on his huge novel *Belle du Seigneur*, which is the ultimately tragic story of a wild, ultra-passionate love affair and its unhappy conclusion — speaking of Cohen and whether he was "Proustian" or not, reminds me of an amusing story about him. I used to go to see him in Geneva. In those days I'd go to visit him on Saturdays in the little apartment he had in the Avenue Krieg, which he never left. We used to talk about him, about Israel, about women, about Ariane, the heroine of his novel, about the way *Belle du Seigneur* ends, with a double suicide, about other possible endings. And I remember that on one occasion, speaking of *Belle du Seigneur*, I said that it, along with Proust's *Remembrance*, was the great twentieth-century love story. Whereupon he just looked at me. For a long moment, with an odd expression, he looked at me, he stared. He didn't say a word, he just played with the amber beads he was always fondling. He stood up. He sat down again. A worried, almost sorrowful expression flitted across his face. And then he asked me, in a lost kind of voice, almost childlike: "Why *along with* Proust's

Remembrance?" For my part, I'd thought it a pretty flattering thing to say, but apparently it had hurt his feelings. He couldn't bear the thought of sharing the honor of having written the great twentieth-century love story with *any*one.

F.G.: That's exactly what I always thought he was like.

B.-H.L.: Albert Cohen's is a strange case. Everyone thought he actually was Solal, the hero of his novel, the marvelous, radiant Solal. People used to come to see him as if on a pilgrimage to the shrine of the prototypical seductive male. But, to tell the truth, there were days when he was much more like his low-comedy character Mangeclous than he was like the handsome Solal.

F.G.: That doesn't surprise me either.

B.-H.L.: It did me — it even astonished me. But I shouldn't be telling you this because, of course, I liked him. Despite his little failings, I liked and respected him enormously. Whereas you . . .

F.G.: Yes. Because it's a thing that often happens with writers. Even if in Cohen's case the identification went farther than it has in other cases. I know women who actually wrote tender and passionate letters to Solal, via Cohen.

B.-H.L.: I've seen some of those letters. I may even say that I've read some of them. Because he was also a fairly indiscreet man: He had an old wooden box in which he kept the letters you're talking about, and he was perfectly willing to get them out and show them —

especially if they'd been written by someone well known. If those women only knew . . .

F.G.: So, you see!

B.-H.L.: That being said, there's another side to jealousy — I almost said "another advantage" — and that's that it's an extraordinary tool for gleaning knowledge. The jealous person's radar is always on. Every system of detection is always working full blast. The attention he pays the world increases tenfold, his capacity for being alert is expanded. A person is never as subtle, never sees or hears so keenly and so much, as when he's prey to that subtle, fecund jealousy Proust praised so highly. Everything has significance for the jealous person, and since everything for him is a sign, he becomes enormously, monstrously alert and lucid.

F.G.: Or completely crazy in the way he reconstructs reality. The fecundity of jealousy . . . It often leads to real crimes. And above all, it's unquenchable because it can live on almost nothing, at least in the extreme cases. Never fall in love with a violently jealous man or woman if you don't want to be persecuted on a daily basis, and with great refinement — that would be my first advice to anyone, if giving advice ever made any difference.

B.-H.L.: It's a perpetual inquisition, an endless grilling — suspicions, boundless curiosity, subtle questions to throw you off guard, traps, little tricks, feigned indifference . . . "Of course you can go, I feel fine this morning, don't worry, go ahead . . . I'm not jealous. No, no, do I look jealous? I look fine, perfectly fine, don't I?"

F.G.: Yes, that's very much what it's like.

B.-H.L.: And then comes the violence. First, of course, it's the imagination, in the strictest sense. The great gift — or vice — of the truly jealous is their awful ability to fabricate pictures in their minds. And then comes the violence, the violence that breaks out when the calm and reasonable tone you've adopted leads your partner to make the fatal mistake of letting slip some tiny admission, whereupon you become violent, first toward the partner and then toward yourself — hatred of the other person and hatred of yourself, which is how jealous scenes generally culminate. I know a man who is jealous. In his paroxysms of jealousy he will beat his head against the wall, against a door, a tree — anything, so long as it's something good and solid that will cause pain and as long as it's convenient to his head. "There," he'll say to his girlfriend after he's given himself a good bashing, with blood running down his forehead, "is that what you wanted? Is that it?" And the poor girl will cry her eyes out because she feels punished by the pain he's caused himself.

F.G.: Good Lord, beating your head against the wall! Even Proust didn't go that far.

B.-H.L.: No. But he was quite aware of the power jealousy can unleash. As you know, he even went so far as to say that literature could not exist without jealousy.

F.G.: Because there would be no literature without love . . . we come back to that.

B.-H.L.: Yes. And because, once again, jealousy sharpens all the senses. A philosopher would say that it produces both itself and the Other, the single and the multiple — it creates a world that's unbearable but, in a way, more vivid.

F.G.: The astonishing thing about jealousy is its durability. You've really been in love with a man, a woman; you separate, you lose track of each other; one day you run into each other again and he or she makes some gesture of tenderness toward whoever they're with, and it's like you've been stabbed.

B.-H.L.: There I don't follow you — or at least, I don't feel things in the same way. On the contrary, it's my impression that when love goes, something vanishes along with it. That's normal, isn't it? Jealousy is a part of love, so it goes when love goes.

F.G.: I think it can survive it for a long time. At least it lives on in the person who keeps on loving after the other person has stopped, the one whose love is dead.

B.-H.L.: Well, Françoise, now we're really getting into deep water. Does a person continue to love when the other person has stopped?

F.G.: Both fires don't go out at the same time, all of a sudden, on cue. That would make things too easy.

B.-H.L.: Can a person love unilaterally?

F.G.: Of course, at least for a while.

B.-H.L.: It's always the same thing: Isn't love always more or less reciprocal? Isn't that an illusion that it somehow requires?

F.G.: Are you joking?

B.-H.L.: Proust, obviously, was very pessimistic about it. He says love is *never* reciprocal. Never. You remember, it was even the basis for the fight he had with that relative of Bergson's, Emmanuel Berl — George Painter told about it in his biography, and then Berl himself did so in 1956 in a book called *Présence des morts*.

F.G.: Yes: Berl had written Proust a fan letter from the trenches and they'd corresponded, and then when Berl was home from the front on sick leave, he visited Proust and told him about being torn between his mistress, his fiancée, and a mysterious girl named Sylvia. Proust expounded his theory of human solitude and the emptiness of human love, but Berl returned to Sylvia.

B.-H.L.: And then, when he told Proust the good news and announced that two human beings can indeed find love together, Proust went into a towering rage. "You're stupid," he screamed, "stupider than Léon Blum!" and he ended up throwing his slippers at him.

F.G.: When he came to write about it, Berl painted a magnificent portrait of Proust, with his "head like a cornered satrap's, his heavy pale cheeks."

B.-H.L.: Berl had always thought that it was his "lack of attraction to homosexuality" that had been the "unsurmountable barrier" between him and Proust, whereas the real barrier, the real difference between them, was his belief in the reciprocity of love, that the true union of human hearts was possible.

F.G.: He wrote a novel, *Sylvia*, about it.

B.-H.L.: Well, we're not obliged to agree with Proust *all* the time. And on this point I don't think I do.

F.G.: Let's say that there's always one member of a couple who loves a little more than the other.

B.-H.L.: But he doesn't always know it.

F.G.: Do you think so? In any event, when it comes to jealousy, men and women are on a par, they're both equally vulnerable to it, equally devastated by it, sometimes equally misguided. And when it comes to this vile kind of suffering, there's always some pompous idiot to say: "How can you suffer because of that man, that woman, when children are starving in the Sahara?" Nowadays neither jealousy nor its companion, love, is fashionable. You can barely mention it — perhaps a word, a sentence, a brief reference in passing. If you're well mannered, you suffer in silence. That's all I really started to say.

B.-H.L.: And it's what we've been disproving for an hour now. Would we have had so much to say, and with such heat, about a truly old-fashioned emotion?

F.G.: It's not the emotion that's old-fashioned. Here again, it's the expression of the emotion that's become more limited, restricted. The emotion will never disappear.

5

On Love As Heaven and Hell

F.G.: Guess what? I dreamed that a jealous man kept me awake half the night. And I kept saying to him: "But I'm transparent, my life is an open book!"

B.-H.L.: And you were lying to him. Amorous relations are never transparent.

F.G.: Probably.

B.-H.L.: People in love think that they know each other, that they understand each other almost without having to say a word. The poor creatures think that theirs is a kind of blessed union, totally harmonious. Whereas . . .

F.G.: Because what they're seeking is union, wholeness, fulfillment. Of course it doesn't exist, or only very briefly just after they've first fallen in love, when they're still in that state of passionate implosion. But they soon begin to grow opaque to each other.

B.-H.L.: It's like the famous Berl-Proust situation we were talking about yesterday. Berl believed in the true union of human hearts, that harmonious, shared desire could exist. He returned to Sylvia and announced, "Glory alleluia, it's a miracle, we're two human beings and we're in love, two bodies as one, love's grace has instantly filled in the abyss that once separated two creatures!" And Proust became enraged and threw Berl out. And there, I find myself once again on Proust's side. Definitely on his side.

F.G.: And yet, the illusion exists . . . Berl's illusion, and the illusion Proust certainly must have cherished, if only for a moment, that love can give us access to another person, whereas in actuality he will always be, and you will always be, forever strangers. To put it another, more pretentious, way: One's partner is possessed of an infinite otherness, even the partner to whom one has felt the closest, to whom one has felt joined as one . . . that old dream. Seeking the true, primal union.

B.-H.L.: I don't remember who said, "Loving means becoming one — but the question is, *which* one?"

F.G.: That's funny.

B.-H.L.: As a matter of fact, I dislike stories of union, of primordial and recaptured oneness.

F.G.: It's not a question of disliking or not disliking. We all cherish this dream, and at the same time it can't be realized.

B.-H.L.: Right.

F.G.: And there's also a basic misunderstanding about amorous relations, namely, that the woman is seeking a particular person and that the man is seeking the femininity — the sex — that will ensure his virility.

B.-H.L.: What makes you think that women seek a particular person and men some abstract femininity?

F.G.: What makes me think it? My profound wisdom.

B.-H.L.: Mine mustn't be so deep, then. Because I seem to know men who are very eager to be with a particular woman, an individual woman, a person. And many women who feel otherwise. Well, we're not going to choose champions to fight that battle for us.

F.G.: Right. But I would like to spend some time on this question of the partner's otherness. However, we mustn't be too heavy-handed about it.

B.-H.L.: No.

F.G.: A couple that know themselves, in the true sense of the word, in which each knows the other and where there are basic areas of agreement, and in which there is mutual pleasure in lovemaking, such couples do exist!

B.-H.L.: Of course.

F.G.: And sometimes — rarely but sometimes — they endure.

B.-H.L.: Without a doubt.

F.G.: So we do agree on that?

B.-H.L.: Of course we do. What I have trouble with is this story of harmony, of some primitive and lost union. It's a notion that started with the Greeks and gradually contaminated all of Western romantic literature. To the point that even today . . .

F.G.: But don't you think it's a beautiful image, that image of the divided, separated entity in search of its lost other half? It's no accident that it's lasted throughout the centuries since the time of Plato. And it has the advantage of being both physical and emotional.

B.-H.L.: No, I don't think it's at all beautiful. I think that those gross bloated creatures with both sexes in one body and one soul, who spend their entire existence in search of their lost androgyny, are the silliest thing Plato ever came up with.

F.G.: The body can have a really intense desire to melt into and join with and sink into another body. Georges Bataille, to whom you often refer and who is hardly a Romantic, made "fusion" the core of his desire, the divine illusion.

B.-H.L.: He says that in another context, thank God. And he never tries to tell us that an androgynous creature lies dormant within each of us!

F.G.: Robert Musil too, in *A Man Without Qualities*, has a good description of "the desire for a double of the opposite sex who resembles us totally while still being another, for a magic creature who will be us but still enjoy an autonomous existence." According to him, the great and lasting romantic passions all begin when someone imagines that he sees his most secret inner self peering out from behind the curtain of another person's eyes.

B.-H.L.: I must not have the same notion of "great romantic passion." If I had to describe it, I would say just the opposite: Love is never so strong as when you are confronting someone different from yourself, someone who is a total stranger to you — the very opposite of this accomplice double, this inverted image, this reflection.

F.G.: Have you ever fallen in love at first sight, Bernard, been overcome with passion? There's always something unforgettable about the very first moments of a passionate affair, something that probably reflects this illusion of becoming One.

B.-H.L.: No, that's not it. What's striking about love at first sight is the other person's strangeness, her overwhelming strangeness. And that's what one remembers with such nostalgia afterwards.

F.G.: No, not at all. What's striking about love at first sight is the impression of finding yourself, that feeling that you were destined for each other since the beginning of time.

B.-H.L.: Too romantic . . . You're definitely too romantic.

F.G.: "Romantic" — I don't think so. What I'm trying to describe is a very widespread feeling.

B.-H.L.: I've never had the feeling I was "made for" anyone. On the contrary, for me, "love at first sight" entails meeting someone radically different from myself, it's the feelings that difference creates, the impression that the other person is — how shall I put it — essentially unimaginable, and that the pleasure she will provide you will therefore be endless.

F.G.: Do you think, as did the Prince de Ligne, that the best thing about love is falling in love and that one should therefore fall in love as often as possible?

B.-H.L.: You could put it that way. But only if you add — a modification that may surprise you — that it's also not a bad idea to fall in love again and again, often, with the same person.

F.G.: A pretty idea. I'll go along with that. But then you won't have that feeling of total difference that seems to set so many men off — and about which you were telling me just a second ago.

B.-H.L.: Not necessarily. Because the other, as I said, is strange. Strange *in essence*. And you can therefore spend an entire life exploring her strangeness.

F.G.: That's sophistry. You're playing with words.

B.-H.L.: No, I don't think so. But that being said, there's another pleasure that many people in love experience, a pleasure that your reference to the Prince de Ligne has reminded me of, and that's the pleasure — if, as he says, the best thing about love is falling in love — of evoking and returning to the enchantment of that moment over and over again.

F.G.: Oh?

B.-H.L.: There's the face that you now know so much better, the body that has become more familiar, the look,
the smile, all of which have grown imperceptibly —
or why not even profoundly — different. And the
pleasure that consists in suddenly shutting your eyes
for a moment and going back in time and trying to
recapture the person, both the same and now
changed, that the woman you love was at the moment you met her — before anything had yet happened, when she was still a stranger to you and
when you didn't yet know whether she would ever
be yours or not . . .

F.G.: That's a very feminine discourse you're using — talking about beginnings, the enjoyment of recapturing
the past, that touch of melancholy. Women are the
ones who love in a melancholy way. "I'm happy but
I'm sad," as Mélisande says. So men in love, men who
are loved, always seem to have sprouted wings, they're
ready to take on the world. Who was ever more in
love than Napoléon Bonaparte?

B.-H.L.: I'm trying to understand this matter of "strangeness." I agree about the classic strangeness, the
strangeness of a new "conquest." That is, you have
this dreamed of, guessed at, desired body — and then
all at once you're actually holding it in your arms. But
there's another kind of strangeness that is at least as
emotional, and that's the kind that persists, even with
a woman you know or think you know.

F.G.: Yes.

B.-H.L.: Well, that's the one I'm interested in at the moment. That's the one I was trying to talk to you about. And that's the one I had in mind when I said, a while ago, that I didn't believe in all this stuff about union, androgyny and so on.

F.G.: I understood what you were saying.

B.-H.L.: You can live for ten, twelve years with a woman, and at times you can feel that in such and such an area you are extremely close to her. But there always comes a time when you discover that she's other, irremediably other. Should one be sorry about that? Should one say "What a pity! What a misunderstanding! How far apart we are"? Of course not. Quite the contrary, that's one of the blessings of love, one of its inexhaustible wellsprings. Love lives on, it feeds on, misapprehensions like that.

F.G.: It feeds on them or they kill it. Understanding each other is getting rid of them, such misapprehensions, to the extent possible, it entails becoming transparent to each other.

B.-H.L.: No, no! Especially not that! On the contrary, that would be the surest way of ruining the whole thing. A couple who have "got rid of" all their misapprehensions is a couple who, quite literally, have nothing left to say to each other. You said it yourself, for that matter: No one can ever be transparent!

F.G.: True. And, of course, that inevitable mystery with which one confronts oneself is a part of love. Sometimes one can discover terrifying things. A gulf can suddenly open up, an abyss, a frightening unknown face, as happens between those lovers who purposely create "scenes," something I detest more than anything, and who in their anger, in their violence, say horrible things.

B.-H.L.: Horrible or not . . . it depends. They can also say very beautiful things. And show a beautiful side of themselves.

F.G.: Come on — those are awful moments, moments in which people no longer resemble themselves.

B.-H.L.: There can be a real pleasure in seeing the other person literally beside himself or herself — in a kind of transport, in a rage.

F.G.: An odd kind of pleasure . . .

B.-H.L.: Just plain pleasure.

F.G.: Followed, true, by wonderful scenes of reconciliation. I know couples who can't live any other way. They may be the ones who know each other best. They live in a continual state of war and derive their pleasure from that, each striving to gain power over the other.

B.-H.L.: Why "gain power"? There's something about "scenes" that reveals desperation. Which makes them more moving.

F.G.: I can't see why.

B.-H.L.: There is. Like a keener form of misunderstanding. An insane desire to force the other person to reveal themselves.

F.G.: You're not going to come out in favor of "scenes"!

B.-H.L.: Why not? Real lovers know that sometimes a good scene is better than a false impression of happiness. We're back to Cohen's Solal. He senses that Ariane is getting bored, and he asks himself: "What kind of scene am I going to create?"

F.G.: That's odious!

B.-H.L.: The most odious, you'll forgive me for dwelling on it, is the charming little ditty: Bodies as one, souls making music together, bodies in harmony, fusion, an idyll."My other half," as the expression goes — and I can think of nothing more obscene than having an "other half."

F.G.: It sounds almost commercial . . . awful! And creating a "whole" — such an illusion!

B.-H.L.: That's why I still prefer love that entails the notion of warring bodies, of bodies at war. We mentioned Greek myth a while ago, the myth — which you found beautiful — of a body once whole and seeking to be reunited. But I'll trade you my Greek myth, which is the one about Eros with his bow letting fly his deadly arrow. Or another, the predatory Eros assailing his beloved, laying siege to her, overcoming her defenses, forcing her to yield, occupying her . . .

F.G.: There's a lot of nuance to what you're saying. As you well know, a couple is not a man *plus* a woman, it's a third entity, which they form together.

B.-H.L.: I don't believe that.

F.G.: And yet it's obvious when you see members of a couple apart and then see them together. We come back to Georges Bataille: "Two beings of the opposite sex losing themselves in each other, forming together a new being different from either of them."

B.-H.L.: I don't want to shock you, but I would point out that there, Bataille, once again, is dealing with a very precise situation. The two creatures do form a new entity, but they do it in bed!

F.G.: Of course. But there's no harm in generalizing.

B.-H.L.: There isn't? I think that you run a great risk when you "generalize" about what happens "there."

F.G.: And yet it's the "truth" of love.

B.-H.L.: It's the ultimate and final situation.

F.G.: It's there that people reveal themselves, that they recognize their own truth.

B.-H.L.: On the contrary, they become unrecognizable — very, very far from what they are.

F.G.: All erotic literature says the opposite. There's Bataille. There's Sade, too, and it's the great lesson he teaches.

B.-H.L.: There's a very simple experiment, one we've all made. You meet a woman — or, if you're a woman, a man — at a dinner party. You look at her. You listen to her. You make a guess at her real face, the one beneath her social mask, the way she'll look later, naked, when she gives in to your desire and you to hers. Well, nine times out of ten you'll be mistaken. You'll get it wrong.

F.G.: I still think that a couple creates an entity in and of itself. Look at your friends. Sometimes you see them separately, sometimes together. Their behavior, obviously, isn't the same.

B.-H.L.: That's something else. You might call it the couple in its theatrical mode: all the things they can't say to each other . . . the front they put up . . .

F.G.: You're confusing real life with its theatrical side. A couple, whether you admit it or not, form a unit, and that unit is a fairly mysterious mixture, a strange combination of molecules.

B.-H.L.: All right, let's admit that.

F.G.: That being said, it doesn't mean that you aren't partly right. There's a whole warlike vocabulary of love. Isn't the other person a "conquest"? Don't you say about some woman, "I've 'had' that one"? Or of a man, "I've done him"? The expressions are pretty ugly, but they're also fairly common. Isn't seduction like overcoming a fortress?

B.-H.L.: If I recall, there's a whole chapter about it in Denis de Rougemont's book *L'Amour et l'Occident*. Wait . . . you have it there. That's the one: the lover "lays siege" to his future mistress. He "overcomes her defenses." He "takes her by surprise." He puts her "at his mercy," and so on. All through that chapter Rougemont is telling us that the West uses the same vocabulary — the same image repertoire — to describe the art of war and the art of love.

F.G.: Yet the whole thing is also very complicated. Because you have to make the difference, don't you? You have conquest, on the one hand — which is an act of war *per se* — and then you have what happens afterward, a life together or, in any case, a shared life.

B.-H.L.: You do? I'm not so sure. That's Rougemont's other theory, I know. It gave rise to a lot of discussion at the time. His view of the incompatibility of love and marriage.

F.G.: In a shared life, Eros no longer has a role. He's let off his arrows, he's deployed his troops; now you have to learn to live in another way, without the poetry and the demonstrations of love you started out with.

B.-H.L.: How sad!

F.G.: Give lovers that, at least . . . that harmony.

B.-H.L.: What I find sad is this notion of two "phases" of love, "conquest" and "shared life together afterward."

F.G.: Sad or not, that's the way it is.

B.-H.L.: Let's go back to Baudelaire again, his relationship with the Duval woman. The beautiful thing about them was that they managed to maintain the same level of violence to the end.

F.G.: "I am the wound and the knife, victim and executioner."

B.-H.L.: Yes. One can imagine a man and woman renouncing lovemaking, over time. Of course, then you have the beginning of a new era — one of peace, harmony, complicity, the whole bag of worms. But if they continue to make love, to desire each other — then the cruelty, the savagery will persist. You cannot deny that aspect of it.

F.G.: It's not only a question of not denying it, you can even seek it out, you can drown in it. But in that case, savagery and cruelty are a matter of mutual consent. You're not enemies, you're accomplices. Do you really think that a couple has to have constant friction?

B.-H.L.: Who's talking about friction? I just think that there's something beautiful about a perpetual discord.

F.G.: Between jealousy, which you deem consubstantial, and war, which you find desirable, love would be hell.

B.-H.L.: But a delicious hell.

F.G.: Maybe, after all, it *is* hell. But with a few wonderful moments of respite, bits of paradise . . .

B.-H.L.: There you are.

F.G.: Indeed, if such moments didn't exist, what couple could put up with the wear and tear of life together?

B.-H.L.: I've never put much stock in this notion of the wear and tear of a shared life, either. But all right. That's another matter.

F.G.: It's the *heart* of the matter.

B.-H.L.: Our real disagreement is with your establishing these different stages. First warfare, then, afterward, a second stage devoted to less violent pleasures. But take Choderlos de Laclos, a warrior among warriors. Do you know what book he was thinking about writing at the end of his life?

F.G.: Yes, I know, but I don't see the relevance.

B.-H.L.: It's this: Here you have a roué, a pervert, an expert in conquests and amorous warfare of all kinds, a twisted man, a bastard, a man whose profession (he was an artillery general, remember) and whose taste and temperament (and what a wonderful life he had, all those international plots and intrigues!) all combined to make it impossible for him to view love as anything other than an endless battle, a war game. And the only idea in his head is to write a sequel to his novel *Les Liaisons Dangereuses*, to be entitled *Les Liaisons Heureuses*, which was to be an apologia for the family, the couple, the simple pleasures.

F.G.: And let me tell you that we mustn't exaggerate "simple pleasures." Between a man and a woman, there's no such thing as simple pleasures. There may be periods in one's life when one aspires to them, as did Laclos in his old age, when ambition or the desire for power, little things like that, can become substitutes for intense, passionate love.

B.-H.L.: Except that I'm not at all sure that the one is a "substitute" for the other.

F.G.: In the old days it was the moment at which men got married and began a family, as one used to put it. They "settled down." We've changed all that. Today, we get married — when we get married at all — very young and not at all with the notion of "settling down," which is pretty ominous, after all.

B.-H.L.: Why can't the two coexist? Why can't you play both roles at once? I rather like the notion of my faithful *and* licentious Laclos, both gentle and belligerent, in love with his Marie Soulanges, who is also growing old, confiding to her his weird plans for his *Liaisons Heureuses* and *also*, without the slightest contradiction, continuing to think like a cocksman and fantasize complicated campaigns of seduction.

F.G.: It's one thing to imagine playing a role and quite another to do it. I don't see Laclos, or anyone else, simultaneously playing the role of a sexual campaigner and that of a lover of the simple life, sitting down to a good home-cooked meal prepared by Marie Soulanges and looking after his little family. No, I truly believe that there is a time for passionate love and another for the kind of love that arises out of other kinds of relationships.

B.-H.L.: What an odd way to look at things.

F.G.: Although it may mean that just when you think you're safe some new passion may spring up and ruin the whole thing. However . . . you don't fall in love passionately dozens of times in your life. Twice, maybe three times . . . At the most . . .

B.-H.L.: I totally disagree!

F.G.: Again!

B.-H.L.: Well, all right: it's late. I suggest a compromise.

F.G.: Compromises are risky things!

B.-H.L.: Basically, there are two main models. First, the idyllic one. The notion, broadly, that you are joined to the other, joined with the other, that two bodies become one and that souls communicate. That's your idea, right? And at the end of the process, there's a moment when union takes place, and that calms the turbulent passions of love.

F.G.: You could put it that way.

B.-H.L.: And then there's the other model, the polemic, warlike model, the notion of continual warfare — or conquest — which there is no reason to stop waging. It's the old notion of courtly love. Expressed another way, it's Baudelaire's idea. To me, it's a more lucid one, but, above all, it's a more exciting one. Not so commonplace, not so banal. One that doesn't follow the somber chain of events — a period of passion followed by a period of calm. Since you're adamant on the point, I'll agree that there's something a bit stiff, a bit unyielding, in this model . . .

F.G.: I'm happy to hear you say so.

B.-H.L.: — and that it too rests on a kind of postulate, namely, there's a wall between lovers, an uncrossable and almost sacred frontier —

F.G.: If I didn't know you were a product of the Ecole Normale Supérieur, I'd have guessed it from the way you've just couched your argument. But forgive me, I interrupted you.

B.-H.L.: We're trying to reach some conclusion — or should we just drop it?

F.G.: No, let's try.

B.-H.L.: The question is: How can we describe the relations between a man and a woman without saying either that "there is a wall between them and that wall is impenetrable" or that "there's nothing between them, they only *seem* to be separated and the consolidation of love will reunite them, in the end"?

F.G.: There you are!

B.-H.L.: Well, my answer is that there may be a third image. And that image is of some gap, or some distance, some space or even, to use a fairly unattractive expression but one that expresses it quite well, a kind of "no-man's-land" that desire sets out to explore. That changes everything, I feel. Because there is a space. It has a content, it has consistency, and, as a result, it is proof against the naïveté of the dream of union. At the same time, it's unstable — it can be traversed, visited, it's a place, by definition, for a thousand voyages or adventures. And it contradicts the depressing image of an iron curtain between people's hearts. There is neither a wall nor a vacuum between my lover and me. There's no eternal misunderstanding or obscene "union" with an "other half." As Daniel Sibony put it, there's an "inter-pair," and it's the infinite space of that "inter-pair" that makes my desire endless.

F.G.: I object to the word "obscene" to describe the union we've been talking about, but aside from that I rather like the notion of a space in which one can move, travel, sometimes stealthily, where one can meet, where desire is replenished. As for knowing why, one day, it ceases to exist . . . that will have to be the subject of another conversation.

B.-H.L.: In any event it allows for the notion that the other person's Otherness can be preserved without their being somehow walled up. Other is other. It will be to the end of time. I shall never be able to violate, or even penetrate, the walls of another's identity. But the other person can sometimes make a breach in those walls, can escape for a moment and, without joining me, at least draw nearer to me.

F.G.: That's very well put. I won't rephrase it, since you are agreeing that at least we come together in the exercise of physical pleasure. We smash the wall before each of us returns to his own otherness.

B.-H.L.: She is she. I am I. But there are some moments in which we, she and I, exist as this "inter-pair" of pleasure, which is neither her territory nor mine, and where we may manage to establish some fleeting contact. I won't go into detail. But isn't that what physical pleasure is? Aren't those the very moments in which erotic pleasure becomes most intense?

F.G.: I'd like to go back a bit. You mentioned Rougemont's famous thesis about the incompatibility of passion and marriage, conjugal love. Do you go along with that, or are you against it?

B.-H.L.: No, no, I'm against it. For that matter, I'm not even sure that Rougemont himself . . . What does he really say, exactly? Isn't there a new edition of his book with a new preface in which he says he was misunderstood and that that's not what he wrote at all? I don't seem to remember.

F.G.: No, he didn't deny it. Briefly, if I understood him correctly — and it's been a long time — he says that passion is always tragic, that passion means suffering, subjection, the burden fate puts on a free, responsible person. That it's to love love more than the love object. He uses Tristan as an archetype, and he says that passionate love represents a radical condemnation of marriage because their origins and their end results are mutually exclusive. He says: "Love as it is conceived of today, that is, passionate love, is the pure and simple negation of the marriage supposedly based on it." And he goes on: "It's not divorce that's become too easy, but marriage, because of our agreement that love is sufficient basis for it notwithstanding conventions of social status, education, fortune . . ." Of course I'm paraphrasing.

B.-H.L.: Frankly, I don't really have a fixed opinion with regard to marriage. I'm not fanatically for it, I'm not fanatically against. Do you think we have to talk about it? Take a stand?

F.G.: We don't *have* to do anything. But we can't just brush it aside when we're supposed to be discussing relations between men and women. It's basic.

B.-H.L.: Fine. If it's basic, we'll talk about it tomorrow.

6

On the Erotic As a Component of Marriage

B.-H.L.: Well then: Marriage. On the whole, and if only to be contradictory, I am going to speak in favor of marriage. The arguments against it are so conventional, so banal in their conventionality. . .

F.G.: Well, I won't defend it. Excepting in a very precise situation: when you marry to have children, to start a family, when that is the purpose of the marriage. If not, the thing I hate about marriage is cohabitation, sharing a bathroom, the slovenliness you often have to put up with, the abrasiveness that's created by a thousand little things. The other person is always on the telephone, they're messy, whatever . . . I want — or rather, I always wanted — to preserve, jealously, some zones of solitude, the illusion, at least, of freedom you have when you don't have to be together, automatically, every evening, when you have to make appointments . . . I used to try to make every evening like a new rendezvous. I think that if you can manage it on the material level, you should resist the temptation to live with someone with all your strength.

B.-H.L.: All the same, you're not going to tell me that you've never . . .

F.G.: Lived with a man? Of course I have. I was married for ten years. But with the others, all the others, I've always avoided it. Even if they've sometimes had trouble understanding my unwillingness.

B.-H.L.: Well, I can't remember ever having lived alone. I've moved from houses to hotels to other houses to hotels when I was between houses. I've lived in Paris, I've lived outside Paris. In other words, it's been my fate — fortunate or not, time will tell — to have been able to experiment with all the countless ways you can "share" in a woman's life. And you'll forgive my saying that never — yes, I believe I can say never — have I experienced the things you describe, that millstone of communal life, that "abrasiveness" of a thousand little things, those problems with the toothbrush, the bathroom. No matter how far back I go, even including the "nomadic" or "poor" periods of my life when economic reasons forced me to live with someone in a really tiny space, those things never really bothered me.

F.G.: The bathroom is only a detail . . . but the feeling of being stuck with each other, that's not. I need room to breathe. And when I found myself on too short a leash, I broke away. And yet he was a very well brought up husband, he didn't make a thing of it. It was just that that's what marriage is: You're never apart. I can see that some people might like that, but I just couldn't. So I've no idea what might have happened if I'd had to live like so many people do nowadays, in a drawer. Yet I know couples who can put up with that kind of permanent intimacy very well, that unremitting dependency in which even having dinner separately becomes an occasion, an event. There must be something peculiar about me.

B.-H.L.: No, you're not peculiar. At the risk of shocking you, I must confess that it's my impression that the trend today seems to be going in your direction. There was a time, of course, when marriage was the norm. People who were always complaining about the prudent bourgeois mind and its limitations were really speaking against marriage itself. It was viewed as the third-rate institution par excellence, as conventional behavior of the worst kind, as the embodiment of all that was worst about the "bourgeois mentality." What does today's bourgeois mentality consist of? There's still the same prudence, it still casts the same chill over things, there's the same cautious attitude, the circumspection with regard to their actions, their words, their commitments. Excepting that that circumspection has switched sides and that it's now preached by the kind of people who preach prudence, independence, vigilance, with everyone in his own niche alone, his own place.

F.G.: The prevailing attitude . . . It's been a long time since I've shared it, and I couldn't care less. I don't see what's so chilling about taking marriage seriously if you decide to enter into it.

B.-H.L.: That's what I was saying.

F.G.: It *is* serious. Divorce means hurting someone, and it always means hurting yourself, and it's a different kind of hurt from the one you get from merely breaking up.

B.-H.L.: I'm saying I agree. But that doesn't stop me from thinking, on the other hand, that in the present-day antimarriage atmosphere there's something — "Oh Lord, the risks! Why take all those risks?" — that's not very attractive.

F.G.: I suppose that my repugnance for cohabitation has a very different origin. It probably comes from the fact that my father died when I was very young. I never knew what it was like to have a man around the house . . . the space a man fills, the attention — or lack of attention — one has to be given, the unshaved chin and ragged pajamas at breakfast, the "Don't forget to leave me some money," the "Play quietly, children, Daddy's tired," or he's working, the "But where's my white shirt, why isn't it ironed, no, not that one!" For me, a man in the house has always been a special occasion, not routine. And I don't like having my special occasions spoiled.

B.-H.L.: As long as we're being frank, you asked me the other day — if I recall correctly, it was even your first question, that first day — whether I liked women.

F.G. Yes. I'm still wondering.

B.-H.L.: I don't remember what my answer was. I probably made some clumsy, embarrassed response. It's always a little odd, don't you think, to just say: "I like women . . ."

F.G.: That's exactly what you said.

B.-H.L.: Well, here's my real answer. Yes, I do like them. I like them enormously. And it's because I like them enormously that I've never been able to live other than extremely close to them. You were talking about daily life, the little drawbacks of daily life. Fine. But I like them too! Sometimes I'm almost overwhelmed by it! A woman taking a bath, a woman getting dressed, a woman making up her face. . . . Ever since I was a child, I've found the idea of a woman making up her face exciting . . . not to mention other things, all the other things — up to and including the most private, intimate details, the things "she" will go to great lengths to conceal from you and which you nevertheless suspect.

F.G.: That's a pretty picture.

B.-H.L.: It's not just a picture.

F.G.: Here, I totally agree with you. If I were a man, I would find intimacy with a woman entrancing, because of her perfume, her way of arranging her hair, her lingerie, even what you call the most private, intimate details. But that's just it: a man is not a woman. And, at least in my opinion, intimacy with a man is nothing like that. It's not that a man's shaving is disgusting, of course, but neither is it particularly exciting, or aesthetic. If he's very handsome, then maybe in the shower . . . but even then . . . A naked man can easily become ridiculous when he's not in the full flush of his manhood. No, it's really not the same thing. I think I like men in the same way as you like women. They often move me by doing something disarming, something vulnerable that makes a contrast to the strength they emit, but I don't like their smelling of cigars . . . even if I bravely put up with it out of respect for their freedom.

B.-H.L.: There, my dear Françoise, I've nothing to say. Other than that I hold to the notion that there's something erotic about what we call everyday life. But I may be wrong, after all . . . Perhaps that's a male notion.

F.G.: I think it's more a personal thing. And talking about it has made each of us reveal more than we usually do. Well, that's what conversation is all about.

B.-H.L.: Yes, but with an underlying idea, after all. I don't say that to "excuse" some undue confidence, but underneath what we're each saying there are two different ideas of eroticism. At least, that's how it seems to me.

F.G.: What do you mean?

B.-H.L.: For me, eroticism always involves a subtle play of the invisible and the visible, a revealing and a concealing, extreme reserve and sudden nakedness. You have modesty, reserve, playacting, whatever you like — and then, all at once, without warning, you have immodesty, obscenity.

F.G.: We're back to Barthes: "Is not the most erotic portion of a body where the garment gapes? . . . It is intermittence . . . which is erotic: the intermittence of skin flashing between two articles of clothing . . . between two edges."

B.-H.L.: There you are! Well, in that connection I don't set too much store by your "evenings that are like rendezvous." That's too "planned" for me, too stagy. There's not enough room for the rest of it, for all the mistakes, all the forgetfulness, all the unexpected physical intrusions, the corporeal side of desire. And as for daily life — what you call "cohabitation" — the good thing about cohabitation is that of course "the woman" does continue to perform, does continue to act, to play a part. She sets out to convince me — or maybe herself? — that, save at moments of transport, of ecstasy, of excess, the body is only a decoy, physiology is nothing but an illusion. In other words, she will play tricks, she'll maneuver and plot, she'll act out for me — and I'll act out for her — a little play designed to make me think her mind's concentrated on higher things . . . and then will come the moment — and it's a moment that always makes me catch my breath — when some word, some little thing, some sign from the soul or the body, some fleeting gesture or pose, will give her away and reveal to her lover — also, in this case, her spouse — that the body does indeed exist and that nature will take its revenge if you try to ignore it. Here too, I'm a confirmed disciple of Bataille. Eroticism demands the maximum of playacting, of ritual. With — and these aren't always programmed — an occasional obscene touch.

F.G.: I don't see two contradictory notions of eroticism in what we've been saying. "A rendezvous every evening" means: Neither person has the right to say that they're complacent, the right to feel that they own the other person, that they're sure that he'll *automatically* be there tomorrow evening on the pretext that we're married. The pact has to be renegotiated on a day-by-day basis. But there's no set time for the erotic. "How fleeting and furtive is the moment of pleasure!" holds true for any time, day or night. Not cohabiting doesn't mean that one forgoes spending lots and lots of time together, sometimes you even work together, and it's then that what you call "an occasional obscene touch" often appears like a flash of lightning.

B.-H.L.: I'm not arguing in favor of the "totally secure"

couple, nor of any "automatic" presence. I'm just speaking in praise of daily life. I do believe that there's a hymn of praise, an erotic one, to be raised in favor of daily life.

F.G.: All right. But in that case there's still the problem of marriage. I don't see how you can continue to be "in favor of" marriage.

B.-H.L.: I don't know why not.

F.G.: Because, if you'll forgive my saying so, you've failed with two.

B.-H.L.: I certainly don't have the feeling that I've "failed" in any way at all.

F.G.: Fine.

B.-H.L.: It's the Clavel story, you know. He had an old friend named Charles Verny, whom he stopped seeing from one day to the next. Françoise Verny, who was a friend of both of them, stepped in. "Charles is sad, he doesn't understand why you're angry." Clavel: "Charles got a divorce; I'm a Catholic, I can't remain friends with a man who's been divorced." Françoise: "Are you kidding? You've been divorced three times, and now you've suddenly become all moral!" To which Clavel replied, drawing himself up: "Yes, but remember: my case isn't at all the same. I didn't become a Catholic until after my third — and last — divorce."

F.G.: Well, let me congratulate you then, a bit prematurely, on your *third* marriage.

B.-H.L.: That's not the point. I'm not Catholic, nor am I about to be. But this bachelor talk, this bachelor ideology men seem to have really gets to me. We were talking about Huysmans the other day. I don't know which of us brought him up . . .

F.G.: You did. Everyone is familiar with Des Esseintes, the hero of Huysmans's *A Rebours*. But you're right. There's always something sneeringly unpleasant about an ideological bachelor, apart from his stupidity. To put it simply, for centuries marriage has been based on values — social constraints, religious constraints, the "crime" of adultery — which have almost ceased to prevail. Thus, we've reached a point where we may well wonder: "What, in the end, is the purpose of marriage?" Of course, everyone is free to proffer his own reply.

B.-H.L.: It's not only Des Esseintes . . . or even Huysmans. There's a whole group of people who have taken this criticism of the married state as doctrine. Balzac did, obviously, but the Goncourt brothers did as well. And Flaubert. And even Zola. And all of them — or at least some of them — exhibit this mixture of heartiness, of off-color joviality, and a very narrow concept of what they call "the single life." It was a very "Champagne Charlie" era, a time when there were debates — in public, if possible — on the question: Can a true artist marry, does he have that right, if he does won't he be frittering away his creative energy, his substance? You may say that all that reflects a fairly healthy reaction to the model, the conjugal model, that prevailed at the time, and I agree. But everything is different today. Conjugality, the poor thing, has been thoroughly discredited. Yet the bachelor discourse, on the contrary, continues to flourish — with all its staleness, its second-rate ideas, its fixations.

F.G.: Balzac and the rest, all those witticisms about adultery and ménages à trois, all that is really from another century. It's gone the way of fortune-hunting men. I see no point in our wasting our time on it. Is the bachelor discourse really still around today? It probably is, since you say so. I've never heard even a hint of it . . . other than among young women who came of age with the student uprisings of May 1968, all of whom turn up their noses at matrimonial commitment. And I know a lot of unmarried men, men living in what might be called common-law marriages, who woke one fine day to find they had lost a child because their companion had gone off and taken it with her . . . and who were very upset about it. Indeed, that kind of man makes a very bitter bachelor.

B.-H.L.: "Young women who turn up their noses at matrimonial commitment . . ." are you sure about that?

F.G.: Oh, not all of them, of course. But the ones who have a profession, or who've already had one or two fairly happy experiences and who don't have their sights fixed on marriage as if it were some kind of rabbit. Do

you know how many children were born out of wed-
lock in 1990? Two hundred and thirty thousand! That
gives you some idea of the number of purposely ille-
gitimate couples.

B.-H.L.: It's like the other day, with the history of sexual
freedom . . . we really don't know the same women.
All the ones I meet, the ones I see now or those I used
to see, seem more or less set on marriage — whether
like aiming at a rabbit, I don't know. But thinking
about marriage, dreaming about it, dreaming about
what it — the illusion of it? — its eternity, might mean:
that they do.

F.G.: That's completely normal. I'm only saying that marriage is no longer the sole goal, the sole preoccupation,
the sole ambition in a girl's life, as it was for such a
long time. I think that's obvious.

B.-H.L.: I wonder if, in fact, we haven't been circling around
the same question for a while now.

F.G.: Which one?

B.-H.L.: In the end, what is the argument of those people
who distrust marriage? At the beginning you mentioned Rougemont, his notion that the ends were
incompatible, that love means passion and that marriage excludes passion.

F.G.: No. In Rougemont's language, passion is not love. It's
just one version of it, in a way a deadly one, one that
fascinates, whereas true love, contented love, has a
bad reputation.

B.-H.L.: It's an age-old argument. You say we're no longer
living in the nineteenth century. Fine. But what you're
saying couldn't be more nineteenth century. We favor
marriage for social reasons, ultimately almost for reasons of health. That's "proper" marriage, "prophylac-
tic" marriage, the marriage that saves you from
sinking into the mire, from going with prostitutes, all
those things. But at the same time, we hold marriage
in contempt. We downgrade it as much as we can. It's
a false, ugly life — from which you are torn by the
storms of passion.

F.G.: Now what are you trying to say!

B.-H.L.: Let's try to put it another way. The idea is that passion can only be temporary, that it wears out, becomes
exhausted, and that it is therefore incompatible with
the timespan of marriage. Well, that's what I thought
you were saying. Am I wrong? Weren't you? I, for one,
don't believe that. I don't believe that passion is necessarily fated to exhaust itself.

F.G.: Well, if you prefer, let's say that it burns out. Sometimes all of a sudden. Yesterday you were accusing me
of being "romantic." You're not going to sit here today
and tell me that a great passion is eternal! In myths,
death settles the question — can you imagine Tristan
and Isolde growing old together after she'd had three
children?

B.-H.L.: Why not?

F.G.: In real life, it's the actual passage of time that exhausts desire and gives rise to a new desire, a desire for another love object. We lack the word for what Rougemont described so well: There is a kind of love that's composed not of passion but of inclination, of tastes and common interests in the broadest sense, of a willed tenderness, of fidelity, even if it's sometimes difficult, a love that just grows deeper, one that doesn't fade, and for which we have no word. And it's on that kind of love, sober and thoughtful, that successful marriage is based, not on passion. Indeed, I find that young people nowadays understand that, or at least many of them do. They don't get married, not right away; they live together, sometimes for several years, before committing themselves. This has become possible because girls no longer have this urge to marry, the old fear of being "left on the shelf." And it's a great change.

B.-H.L.: I'm not romantic. Or I try not to be. And I have known, and known well, enough attachments that haven't worked out for me to be very, very prudent. But I'm not saying that they "wore out." Nor that passions "burn out." It's not only that those expressions are ugly ones — because that's still important, isn't it, the ugliness of an expression? — it's the notion itself that I take exception to. Because the idea is the same in both cases. First, you say that passion "burns out" — you're envisioning it as a kind of flame, a candle, with a limited burning capacity. Then you say that it "wears out" — and it's like an old rope you keep pulling on until you get it to break. Common to both is the fact that, in your view, passion, your kind of passion, is a kind of thing, a commodity, with all the disparaging connotations those words have. There's a domain of different loves, a preserve in which you go hunting. You fire. You fire again. And one fine day you've brought them all down, there aren't any more. You've emptied your passion like you empty a bank account. Well, I don't believe that. I don't at all believe that that's how things happen.

F.G.: I don't think of passion as a "commodity" that can be used up, or like a flame that burns out. Burnt out . . . it's a bad expression, you're right, even if it is Proust's. But I can't think of a better one to say that one day it ends, boom! — it falls apart, it disappears, whatever. It was there, and now it isn't.

B.-H.L.: But the question is: Why? Yes, why was it there and why isn't it there any longer? Why do you stop loving? Why do the ties loosen? People say, "It's inevitable." You yourself say, "Passion is not eternal." And if you're so sure that passion cannot last, it's because you really do believe in these stories of erosion, exhaustion, disenchantment. But I don't. I'm well aware that people break up, that people part. But I don't think it's because they "tire" of each other.

F.G.: No. Again, if there's truly passion, I don't believe you "tire" of it. And if I say that external passion doesn't exist, that one day you somehow awaken from it, it's not because I have some theory about it, it's merely an observation. I know that it's unacceptable if you yourself happen to be caught up in some passionate affair, I know that you can imagine anything except the fact that someday it will no longer inhabit your whole heart, all your emotions — such a thing is absolutely unimaginable. And yet one day it is over. And when it's over, for a woman, when she's the one who's broken it off, she can easily become hard. It seems to me that men get out of things more . . . politely, less harshly, sometimes they even feel remorse, but I may be wrong. However, you look like you know why things eventually end. Tell me, I don't know.

B.-H.L.: I don't "know" either. Who can pretend to "know"? I have some observations, mere observations. And I've also heard stories . . . people have told me things. You know, I wrote a novel, part of which was narrated by a woman. So I've looked into it, I investigated. The whole novel was built on an investigation.

F.G.: I didn't know you had a Paul Bourget side. Excuse me, I'm teasing.

B.-H.L.: Marie Bourget wasn't so bad, not so bad at all. She was a great reader of Stendhal and she inspired Proust, who based some of Odette's characteristics on her. She'll be back in fashion someday, you'll see.

F.G.: Fine.

B.-H.L.: But what were we talking about? The key question
is the sexual question, is it not? That's what we mean
when we talk about exhaustion, about being worn
out?

F.G.: Oh, it's more complicated than that. There are couples
who still "function" very well — if I may use the term
— where that's concerned, but who still fall out of
love, one or the other of them, or both. Usually one
does it before the other one. And falling out of love is
just as uncontrollable as passion. You suddenly notice
that the beauty spot is really a wart.

B.-H.L.: All right. But we're still talking about "that."
People say, "We don't understand each other any
more, it's no longer working, it's not the passion it was
in the beginning." Most of the time what they're really
saying is: "We don't desire each other any more, our
bodies no longer have that attraction, that marvelous
desire for each other."

F.G.: There can be the extinction of desire there too. Desire
has to be worked at, practiced, but extinction can happen fairly soon. But I'm not reducing falling out of
love to such a — what's a good word? — "mechani-
cal" phenomenon.

B.-H.L.: You can put it any way you like. The facts are there.
Days go by, weeks go by, and with each day, with each
week, the invisible barrier that separates two bodies
becomes a little thicker. Every day, every week, leads
them a bit further into the tragic, and anguishing, im-

passe. And the poor creatures are forced to face the facts: Nothing has changed, everything has changed. They aren't enemies, they're strangers. From the outside, there's nothing to indicate their new status, but they know the awful secret, they know how unhappy they have become. Generally, it's the women who break down. They give up, resign themselves; more precisely, they accept — when they don't participate, actively, in its creation — the reassuring version of the situation that they're given. There are books about it. Balzac wrote some of them. In another vein, there's Courteline. It's the old ploy of the headache, of constant fatigue, of bodies that instantly fall asleep, or pretend to fall asleep, as soon as they lie down together. It's the thousand and one pitiful explanations they pretend to go along with, until the day comes when they say: "That's it, enough playacting." And then they revolt. Most often in silence — but they do revolt. Then they take a lover. And then the lover gets the whole thing thrown at *him*.

F.G.: We've come a long way from passion. Now you're talking about the desire that accompanies nearly all unions, at least on the male side. Yes, of course it fades . . . you didn't want to admit that a while ago. And there's nothing more sad than acting as if it hadn't. To have to carry out Albert Cohen's terrible sentence, "Love has been poured out, it must be drunk down." You have to break it off. And at once. Or, if you

get along very well in other ways, if you like living together, if you've formed very strong bonds, then you
each start having affairs on the side. That's another
model, and a relatively common one.

B.-H.L.: Wait a second. We'll come to breaking up and affairs on the side! For the moment, the question is:
What happens when people stop loving each other
and separate, what happens when they stop desiring
each other? What I'm saying has two aspects that I
want to clarify. First, time in and of itself has nothing
to do with it. Time, as time, does not necessarily work
against the perpetuation of desire. It's not that bodies
grow tired of each other, get too used to each other. It's
not that they necessarily lose their mystery, their secret. No, that's not it. That can't be it, because we
agree, do we not, on the notion that desire is a mechanism for exploring that famous "intermediate" space?
and that that space is infinite, and that desire, therefore, must be infinite as well?

F.G.: So what is it?

B.-H.L.: Desire, the infinite, we can't get away from that.
What we have to keep always in mind is that desire, at
its very core, possesses all it needs to maintain itself.
Desire is like Cartesian movement: it is continuous. It
can continue, indeed, forever. If desire were left to itself, if it weren't accompanied, disrupted, interfered
with by other kinds of things, other passions, it would
never flag. The second thing, then —

F.G.: But every desire flags, not just "Desire" with a capital *D!* I can accept your "infinite space," all right. But the other person changes. Every person changes over time. I don't mean only the physical changes that you barely notice when you live with someone, but more subtle changes. You fell in love with a vibrant young man with no money who wanted to be a writer ... you end up with a desk-bound businessman. You fell in love with an idealistic, fragile girl and you find yourself in bed with someone who's flying a Boeing. And what about you yourself, what have you become? I'm not exaggerating much. You fall in love with a person at a particular moment. And that moment must change.

B.-H.L.: Let me finish. The second aspect is that very "disturbance," that "instability," those "interferences" — all those things that impede the pure play of desire. In short, passions, other passions. The simplest example is that of another woman — or another man — who comes along and replaces the person you loved yesterday.

F.G.: Elementary, my dear Watson.

B.-H.L.: But it can take other forms. For example, with the same person there can be another strong, overriding passion that will interfere with the first one and invade its space. There are couples eaten up by disappointment, or by some vague ill-feeling, some grudge. Or by jealousy, in its pathological form. Or by things having to do with their children, or the arrival of new children. Or by money. Or power. Or by suddenly becoming aware of how the other person looks, or by deception, or by bitterness. Or by the other person's unexpected reaction to some event that you, wrongly or rightly, view as important. In short, there are a thousand possible emotional interferences, a thousand different obsessions — whether ridiculous or not, it makes no difference — that make the other person's body not transparent but opaque, impervious to the old desire. But that body is always there, lovable and desirable. We can even agree that it hasn't changed, nor have you really changed. But between you and it there is now the substance of the new passion and the misunderstanding it has created. Desire hasn't been exhausted, it's been driven away. Passion hasn't "faded," it's been rendered impossible by another passion, which has suddenly replaced it.

F.G.: Yes, I could agree in certain cases with the notion of a passion's being driven out. That's life. A person cannot enjoy or bear their passion alone with their loved one, shut up in a little world of their own. In order to exist, love needs to be witnessed by other people . . .

B.-H.L.: Indeed, there you have the overriding theme of *Belle du Seigneur*. That was Cohen's great idea.

F.G.: May I venture to say that Albert Cohen bores me just a little? At least in *Belle du Seigneur*. When I go back to it I find myself skipping a lot of pages. Nevertheless, the falling-out-of-love episode is masterful. That man, that woman, enclosed together in their passion, who end up gasping for air like fish out of water, the pitiful pretexts they seize on in order to continue to play their roles as marvelous lovers when they're dying of loneliness, Solal the hero's asphyxiation — it's the cruelest thing ever written about the limitations of human love.

B.-H.L.: That's true.

F.G.: But I was thinking of something else. I was thinking of the simple fact that love needs other people to affirm itself, that happiness has to remain "in the world" in order to be realized. This is described briefly and very poignantly in a novel that is far less well known, a novel by Pier Vittorio Tondelli called *Separate Rooms* — a masterpiece. Have you read it? Now there's a writer who has managed to describe love, even if in his case it happens to be love between two men.

B.-H.L.: No, I haven't read it. What's it about?

F.G.: A man, a writer, tells how he fell in love with another man, that's all; he describes, casually but very acutely, how such loves— more so than others — are condemned to a clandestineness that asphyxiates them.

B.-H.L.: It's the whole problem of the back-street love affair. Some back-street affairs last forever, but as a rule they break up. And when they break up it's because of that feeling of asphyxiation. Women — because most often it's the woman — cannot put up with enforced clan-

destineness, secretiveness. They're usually the ones
who break it off, one way or another they break it off —
quite brutally, if they're the brutal type, discreetly,
if that's their nature. Sometimes they manage to
give signals, to leave indications, familiar objects, that
betray the forbidden liaison. At the least, they will see
to it that people know that there's something they're
not supposed to know, that people start to say that
something's going on that mustn't be talked about —
"Shhh! that's a secret, a very precious, very tender secret!" But to accept living in a hothouse, to go along
with utter silence, to resign themselves to melting
away — if only in the heart of the man they love —
without a trace, that is one solution that can never, in
the end, be borne.

F.G.: On the other hand, I'm astonished to see the many
women who are still prepared to act in *Back Street*.
However, all my examples are drawn from women
who are now over thirty. I'm not sure that younger
women are so ready to put up with lonely weekends,
with tearful New Year's Eves, to put up with the
somewhat ridiculous sight of a man who is, when you
come right down to it, really afraid of his wife, even
when he hides his fear behind noble feelings. In any
case, you have to be awfully in love to put up with
being loved in the shadows . . . and for love to with-
stand such underexposure. Love entails not only duration and fidelity of feeling, but publicity. *Back Street* is
a trap for females.

B.-H.L.: I'm not saying there are fewer of them, I'm saying that they never really went along with the back-street game. At least not completely. As I said, they manage to create for themselves a more flattering role than that of some poor girl crying alone on New Year's Eve. And then it's very simple: either the man accepts it, pretends not to notice, agrees to go along, dangerous as it may be, with the game of "secret-liaison-to-be-spoken-of-in-whispers," or he's sent packing back to live his mediocre life.

F.G.: I don't understand what you're trying to say. What "flattering role"? What can be flattering about such a situation, however one puts up with it? Little affectations don't change a thing. Some women in back-street affairs even count on eventually capturing the man they love, they will demonstrate extraordinary perseverance, single-mindedness, craftiness, and sometimes they will even succeed. But that's something else. In such cases you have to pity the man who's being torn apart between two women, even though he should have known better than to get himself into such a mess in the first place. But those sweet, patient, and heroic back-street wives, they really take the cake.

B.-H.L.: Why not . . .

F.G.: Because they are more the objects of condescension than of the admiration you've just voiced.

B.-H.L.: Not at all. If you knew . . .

F.G.: Well, so much the better.

B.-H.L.: I'd like to go back a moment to the basic question.

Why is love so averse to isolation, clandestineness?
Why does it languish when forced to live in a vacuum,
in the "little world" you mentioned a while ago? First,
I'd note that as a general rule people in love say just
the opposite. They say things like: "No, not at all! We
dream of a hidden passion! We dream of being completely alone together! Love is asocial, isn't it? A rebel-
lion against the community. Isn't being lovers like
founding a little community all one's own?" I agree
that they soon change their minds. They change their
tune. But that's what they say.

F.G.: Man is a social creature. He's unable to function as
himself if he never sees anyone else. He suffocates in
solitude, even if it's a shared solitude.

B.-H.L.: If you're right — and I think you are — there are
two explanations. First, there's Alfred Cohen's, which,
I grant you, is fairly curt. He says that lovers get bored
with each other, that they quickly run out of things to
say to each other, that their intimate conversations
become incredibly tedious, their evenings together become endless, their love becomes anemic when deprived of the sustenance it once drew from the great
world outside. They used to curse that world, their
only dream was to escape from it. Now that they have,
now that they are given over exclusively to their love
affair, their only dream is to get out of it again, to
breathe a little.

F.G.: Yes. As I said, it's the most successful thing in Cohen's
book.

B.-H.L.: There's a second explanation. A more valid one, in my opinion. It's based on the notion that the relationship between a man and a woman is never confined to just the two of them. There is one of them, and then there's the other, but between the two of them there is a whole series of "third parties" who are looking in on the erotic game that's being acted out. The mimetic structure of desire. Circularity, mirroring . . . René Girard says something like this, as have many earlier writers.

F.G.: He wrote a book about mimetic desire as reflected in Shakespeare's plays!

B.-H.L.: Yes . . . The shadows in the background, the silent witnesses, the group of more or less clearly defined phantoms that lurk around the lovers. If the theory is correct, if a person can only love in the shadow, the gaze, of others, if there is always a "crowd" present at any amorous encounter, then there you have the real reason why love cannot bear a double solitude. Lovers can go on reciting their little speeches about asocial, untamed love till the end of time, but there are "basic" reasons why it will never work.

F.G.: I think that both explanations are valid at different levels. And that "little worlds," or desert islands if you prefer, can only be paradise for about two weeks at the most.

B.-H.L.: There you're going a bit far!

F.G.: We can't end this chapter without mentioning contingent love affairs. The model, obviously, is the relation-

ship between Jean-Paul Sartre and Simone de Beauvoir, which is a creation in and of itself. De Beauvoir's
creation, principally. But in the end, both of them managed, even when they no longer had any physical relations whatsoever, to preserve a love, a tenderness, a
reciprocal respect, a living, demanding relationship,
what was actually a steadfast fidelity. Whereas at the
same time de Beauvoir was to find with Nelson Al-
gren what she'd never known with Sartre, or with any
other temporary lover, namely, pleasure — and Sartre,
in addition to his girlfriends, was to have a serious
and lasting relationship with the famous Dolores. We
don't know whether Sartre was jealous or not, but de
Beauvoir clearly was. But what bound them to each
other proved to be indestructible. Is that exceptional?
Probably. Is it unique? I'm not sure. Enviable? More
enviable than the continual pursuit of passion inter-
spersed with divorces. Oddly enough, this man and
this woman who rejected marriage ended up by having a successful . . . marriage.

7

On the Pleasures of Fidelity

F.G.: What about fidelity? Is infidelity incompatible with love, should it be admitted, should it be kept hidden? I'd like to hear what you have to say about it.

B.-H.L.: Do you remember what Ernest Renan said? It's at the beginning of his book *Souvenirs d'enfance et de jeunesse*, in which he writes about his youth. He asks to what things a man should be faithful in his lifetime. And his answer is: "To himself, to his publisher, and to one woman."

F.G.: I don't recall that. It's well put. Am I to understand that you agree?

B.-H.L.: What I like about it is "to one woman" — it's being in the singular, its provisionality, one might even say its uncommonality. What I like, if you will, is fidelity that's accidental, that's incidental. The other kind of fidelity, the one based on principle, the kind that is supposed to be a worthwhile end in and of itself, the fidelity of the troubadours and courtly love — in my opinion, that kind (and this may shock you) has nothing to do with love.

F.G.: I'm not at all shocked. I've always wondered about the "proprietorial right" that allows us to deprive a man of any woman, or a woman of any man. It seems a peculiar way of expressing love. Of course in that case you have to work out the protocols, if I may put it that way. Do you tell each other everything? Do you say nothing? Do you pretend not to know, and so on?

B.-H.L.: "Tell each other everything" No! That would be horrible!

F.G.: You recall Malraux's novel *Man's Fate*? When May tells her husband, Kyo, that she's slept with another man, she does so because it's part of their contract of reciprocal freedom, and suddenly that dyed-in-the-wool revolutionary finds himself completely overwhelmed. So what has happened — she's cheated in the true sense of the word?

B.-H.L.: I'm suspicious of contracts between lovers . . . indeed, of contracts in general. You have contracts of fidelity: "I'll be faithful to you; no matter what happens, I'll be faithful to you." There are contracts of infidelity: "Freedom for one, freedom for the other; whatever

happens is accepted and you tell each other everything as you go along." And then there are perverse
contracts, or lewd contracts, like the one in *Liaisons
Dangereuses* between Madame de Merteuil and Valmont: "A contract for joint crime, to be accomplices in
deceit." I can't put it any other way: I loathe the very
idea of a contract, an agreement, between lovers.

F.G.: There are some good agreements. But "telling each
other everything" — I hate that too. Nevertheless, a
person cannot talk as you have about jealousy and neglect infidelity. To start with, where does infidelity
begin? With a one-night stand? Do you give it the
same importance when it's yours or when it's your
lover's?

B.-H.L.: One-night stands . . . Obviously, infidelity begins with
the one-night stand. Men — and women too, some-
times — who tell you differently are talking through
their hats. They're being hypocritical. Or worse —
they're wretched lovers.

F.G.: So you're preaching absolute fidelity?

B.-H.L.: I'm not preaching anything. How could I preach
anything? I'm merely saying that you mustn't take
people — in this case women — for fools. And that
men who say, "No, no, that doesn't count, it was just a
passing fancy! There are times when making love is no
different from having a Coke" — men like that don't
give a damn for other people and, worse, they're bastards.

F.G.: Men aren't the only ones who have encounters that last only a day, or an evening, even if they may be in the majority. The opportunity comes along, the grass is soft . . . To call people who do such things "bastards" — or sluts— is going a bit far. Not that I'm taking their side, but, after all, in love there's always a first time. Some great love affairs have grown out of what was thought to be just a passing adventure at the time.

B.-H.L.: I'm not saying that men are bastards for having a one-night stand. I'm reproaching them for going on to tell about it and say that it just happened, like that, without being planned, and that it's of no importance, that there's love and then there's love, and so on. Believe me, I know what I'm talking about. The only thing that can redeem an unfaithful man is his awareness that he's hurting someone. Whatever the circumstances, however important the liaison, however fleeting, however absurd, it's never experienced with that kind of innocence.

F.G.: Fine. But who said that fidelity had to be such a burden? On men more than on women, true; it's as if men had this constant itch to show off sexually. I think women have more self-control. Do men need to reassure themselves, to have proof that they can be desirable?

B.-H.L.: A "burden." That's not the word I'd use. You can derive pleasure from the practice of fidelity. You can find real enjoyment in being faithful. You don't go around telling yourself, "I'm being faithful," and even less do you say, "I'll be faithful forever." But then, behold, you are. You find that you are being faithful. And being faithful that way, without a contract, without an agreement, being faithful without thinking about it, naturally, does bring with it a kind of pleasure.

F.G.: It's also a pleasure for the person witnessing it. We love examples of human fidelity. We're all moved by it, as we are by a successful work of art, by something beautiful in itself. As for me, I wholeheartedly agree with the pleasure produced by spontaneous, unconstrained fidelity. But, after all, we're not deaf and blind — the least we can say is that such fidelity is hardly the rule. And again I ask you, because you're a man: Why this male passion for "skirt chasing" when at the same time the majority of the chasers maintain that they love their wives or their companions and want above all not to "cause her pain"? There are no statistics available, but it appears obvious that the unfaithful man is a much more prevalent creature than the unfaithful woman.

B.-H.L.: Yes, I do think that women are actually much less unfaithful than they're reputed to be. I'd almost add: less unfaithful than they themselves say they are. Of course, there are "modern" women. There are women who are getting even. There are even women who pretend to be unfaithful. And there are those women who are conforming to what men expect or desire. But as a whole, you're right. Men who truly like women — men who listen to them, who draw them out, who — of course — desire them and love them — are fully aware of this. The proportion of "virtuous" women, for whom an erotic adventure is always a matter of great importance, hasn't changed much with so-called sexual freedom. As for men . . .

F.G.: "A matter of great importance . . ." That's not what I was trying to say. There are many women — modern or not, I don't know what that means — for whom an erotic adventure is *not* a matter of great importance. What I believe is that a woman who is physically happy with a man has no desire to find herself in another man's arms, and that things are completely different with men. Once again, how do you explain that? It would be interesting to know, to understand this urge.

B.-H.L.: There are several reasons for it. First, there's pleasure. Might as well be honest, there's pleasure. The encounter, the seduction, the discovery of a new body, the fantasies that accompany it, the part of yourself that emerges, the *new* part of yourself. Because remember: a seducer is not a whole man, an integrated personality that can go from one woman to another while he himself doesn't change. No. Each conquest delights him. Each conquest reinvents him, makes him into someone else. You might say that each new woman gives birth to another him. Lévinas has beautiful things to say about the caress. He says that caressing a person is not merely touching them, stroking them, enjoying their body. It's also, in a very basic way, fashioning them. There's a lot of that in the Don Juan syndrome, a boundless narcissistic curiosity, a hopeless quest for one's own multiple faces. There's the notion that each adventure is going to provide you, if not with a soul, at least with a feeling, a gesture, an aspect of yourself that you had never suspected. You can call that egotism, selfishness, an aggravated case of egotism. But that's the first reason.

F.G.: And the second?

B.-H.L.: The second . . . Obviously, there are many other reasons. Curiosity, the pleasure of conquest, the thought of throwing out a net, of tracking one's prey, of having it take your bait, there's the difficulty involved or how easy it can be, the fact that it *seems* difficult, that your object eludes you, draws back, seems at the outset unattainable — and then, in the end, turns out to be available. Seducers are odd creatures. They'd love to run up against some obstacle, they wouldn't really mind being disappointed, but they're disappointed that in fact they're so rarely disappointed. And when you add in vanity, or prestige. And there's also a "market" in women, or your "unfaithful" man thinks there is. It's an ugly expression, but it is true that there is a women's "market" and that some men — and I emphasize "some" men, for there are some seducers, and perhaps the most authentic ones, who prefer some kind of secrecy, who like the clandestine — take pleasure in cornering it.

F.G.: Who has such love affairs? In the end, they go on within the same more or less restricted group of people. Without some fortunate or unfortunate accident, it's hard for a person to avoid social, cultural predestination. But even within that group some conquests enhance your credit, others lower it. It's true for women as well as for men.

B.-H.L.: Right. Take your Don Juan . . . It's obvious that in exercising his greater or lesser aptitude for "playing the market" he's competing with other "experts." It's not a very elevating picture, I agree, but, unfortunately, that's the way it is. And that goes for everyone . . . and I do mean everyone.

F.G.: Do you think so?

B.-H.L.: Leaving people who are still alive to one side, take someone like Pierre Drieu La Rochelle, the talented writer who was such a devoted collaborator during the Second World War that he had to commit suicide to escape possible execution after the Liberation. People can't stop wondering why his contemporaries were so nice to him, so indulgent. They were well aware of who he was. They talked to him. They could all read his articles, they knew what he stood for, but they went on liking him, seeing him, spending time with him.

And when I say "they," I'm not talking only about the people who contributed to the German version of *La Nouvelle Revue Française* when he was heading it, I'm talking about men like André Malraux, Paul Nizan, Emmanuel d'Astier de la Vigerie, to mention only three.

F.G.: Even today, people are endlessly indulgent toward him.

B.-H.L.: One day I decided I'd try to understand it. When I wrote, and filmed, my *Aventures de la liberté*, I tried to understand it. And the thing that really stood out was this question of women. Drieu was a man who was knee-deep in women. And that reputation — which was probably exaggerated — fascinated men like Nizan or Malraux and led them to overlook or ignore the rest. With that reputation, what difference did it make if he was a fascist, an anti-Semite? An aura of charm and beautiful women surrounded his name and, in a way, gave him sanctuary. I'm talking now about Drieu, but I could cite other examples, including some closer to home. In every instance, the principle is the same: This purported virtuosity in the art of seduction always plays an essential role in the ascendancy a man exercises over his peers.

F.G.: I'm afraid that you're right on all scores and that there *is* some irresistible aura about what we used to call a "ladies' man." It's the aura of his exploits. And, by definition, he's unfaithful. Yet, at the same time, there's something fascinating about long-term, committed fidelity, something we envy, perhaps without showing it. In his *Journal* Jules Renard wrote: "My being a faithful husband, which is a comic status, bolsters my literary reputation."

B.-H.L.: Is that really true?

F.G.: What?

B.-H.L.: That fidelity bolsters a literary reputation.

F.G.: I think that great fidelity always impresses people. Take the case of Aragon.

B.-H.L.: But take Hemingway, who was just the opposite.

F.G.: Yes, but no one is impressed by Hemingway.

B.-H.L.: What do you mean, "no one is impressed"?

F.G.: It's only his work that's impressive.

B.-H.L.: His work and everything else. He's an outstanding example of the kind of seduction that works on two levels at once.

F.G.: Let's agree that you can "impress" in various ways. By being faithful to a woman and by going off to fight in Spain and because you've shot yourself in the chest.

B.-H.L.: Perhaps . . .

F.G.: Well, since I'm trying to learn something about men, I'll continue with my questions. Here's a basic one: You learn that the woman in your life is having a secret affair. What do you do? According to you, what should you do? Reproach her, pass it off, treat it lightly, keep quiet about it?

B.-H.L.: Leave her.

F.G.: A good decision if you can stick to it. It's sometimes difficult. You suffer. I'd be less radical than you if it were only a one-night thing. There can sometimes be extenuating circumstances. If it's more serious than that, then obviously that's what you should do, leave her. Quickly, a clean break without scenes or tears, but decisively. Break it off. Unless, of course, you'd come to some reciprocal understanding to be tolerant, which is more civilized.

B.-H.L.: Mmmm, I'm not so sure about that!

F.G.: In any event, that's not how things usually happen — at least in the opposite case. Women are taught by their mothers, who learned it from their mothers, that they must learn how to "close their eyes" to things while at the same time "keeping them open," because "you know what men are like." And with more or less good grace, more or less pain, they do overlook his escapades, thereby entering into a process of lying that is degrading for both of them, with the inevitable "But you know that you're the one I really love" that all deceived women have heard at least once. So what's the alternative? Reprisals? A vulgar solution if there ever was one, and one that accomplishes nothing. No, if you can afford to, and that's not always easy, you have to leave, leave, leave. And here's where the modern women about whom you're so cynical are better equipped than they used to be, because they're materially independent. And that changes everything. I know a man, very well known in Paris, who's just had a very cruel experience. His wife left him in ten minutes. He found himself sitting alone in his apartment, totally taken aback by what had happened to him.

B.-H.L.: Yes. I could cite some opposite situations. Femmes fatales, dangerous women, women about whom everyone said, "She'll leave, she'll leave on the spot, I know her and she won't put up with such an insult for a second," and then, when the time comes, nothing happens. Are you saying it's because that's how she's supposed to act, she's been taught to act that way by her mother? Perhaps. But perhaps it's also because of love. A love stronger than pride, stronger than resolutions, stronger than self-determination. I can't think of anything sadder or more moving than that.

F.G.: Believe me, the sight of a man who's trying to hang on, who threatens, who asks for "explanations," that's pretty sad too. This vision you have of women swallowing anything, insult, humiliation, is very odd. Of course such women do exist, and since they're the type of woman you like, they're the ones you've known.

B.-H.L.: I wasn't talking about myself. Or about the ones I've known.

F.G.: I'm not saying that women have suddenly become intransigent with regard to infidelity. Indeed, we ought to make clear which kind we're talking about, a passing affair or an ongoing clandestine relationship. I'm saying that the new women who are financially independent have more strength to break things off when they've been too hurt, too humiliated by being cheated on. And that's a good thing.

B.-H.L.: We always get caught up in the same argument. You're talking to me about women's independence, their financial autonomy, and I'm talking to you about love, maybe even of the pain of love. And it's my belief that one has absolutely nothing to do with the other. How can you not agree? How can you say differently? You yourself — you yourself have been the prototype of such a liberated, independent, free woman. You've made money, you've been in charge of vast undertakings, you've been in control — real control, the kind that means power, not money — of dozens, of hundreds of men. Has that given you — how did you put it? — "more strength to break things off"? Has that given you a greater "invulnerability"?

F.G.: No way! There's no such thing as invulnerability. And as for pain, the pain could kill you. But how can you believe that you'd be the same person if you didn't know where you could lay your head, if you had no autonomous existence in the society, if you were just Mrs. So-and-so or you were nothing, or if, on the contrary, you had something of your own to fall back on? It's not just a question of money!

B.-H.L.: "Something to fall back on" only *seems* to make a difference. There are women who live in fear of being alone, of being thrown over, of being abandoned, no matter what they have to "fall back on." When those women are really abandoned, they all behave in the same way.

F.G.: Wait a minute. Right now we're talking about women who would rather "put up with it" than break things off when they find they're being deceived, is that right? I was the first to tell you that that was the most prevalent attitude. But why do you want to deny that all women aren't cut to the same little timid, sneaky, unhappy pattern you have in mind, the nineteenth-century pattern, not to mention the model of barely fifty years ago? I can't believe that you've never come across a woman who doesn't go off to cry in a corner and who doesn't try to hang on to an unfaithful husband or lover. Unfortunately, I can't name names here, it wouldn't be fitting. But it's not for lack of examples.

B.-H.L.: Examples, counterexamples . . . we could play that game forever. But you don't convince me that women's independence, their financial or professional autonomy, have changed their reactions to such circumstances all that much. You'll forgive me for bringing it up again, but I'd taken a particular example. I asked you if you yourself —

F.G.: Myself . . . I've always ended things cleanly. In the kindest way possible. Without lies. And when I was not the one who broke up, when it caused me pain, I didn't say a word or make reproaches. It was a clean break. However, I never said that being autonomous would spare you suffering, nor that it could help you avoid outrageous behavior! Jealousy plus breaking up equals the possibility that foolish things will happen. But men are just as capable of them as women.

B.-H.L.: Have you done foolish things?

F.G.: You might call them foolish. In such a situation some men and women become terribly vengeful. They become capable of senseless, brutal things. I used to know a woman who, when her lover left her, shot him in the head one night when he was asleep. A very well-bred woman. She's probably still rotting away in prison. Her name was Lea, Lea S.

B.-H.L.: Oh, nobody spends much time in prison for something like that. You're not supposed to talk about it, but nobody spends very long . . .

F.G.: There's a degree of pain that seems to make you mentally blind. This was a beautiful and charming woman, and rich to boot. She would have been just over forty, he was younger than she. She had really shaped him, civilized him. They seemed to form an untouchable couple until he fell in love with another woman. It put her through actual torture. She cried, she howled like an animal, she begged, she tried to plead with her rival — in vain, of course. And then, one evening, she killed him in cold blood. In a way, she was setting herself free.

B.-H.L.: Now, what about you?

F.G.: I killed myself. I punished myself for not being loved any longer. It's a long and uninteresting story.

B.-H.L.: I'm sorry. We won't talk about it.

F.G.: No, please, let's not.

B.-H.L.: But before we separate we should come back to fidelity. I don't think we've exhausted the subject of fidelity.

F.G.: It's inexhaustible.

B.-H.L.: We were talking about "contracts of fidelity." About this admittedly stupid way of saying, "I can change, we can both change, become other people, but we've made an agreement between us, we have a contract of fidelity."

F.G.: Yes, it is naive. Because as a general rule you draw up that contract at a time when your love isn't threatened. It's like the Boy Scout's oath.

B.-H.L.: It's "courtly" fidelity. Rougemont's fidelity . . . the influence of Antoine de Saint-Exupéry. You know his famous description — I'm quoting from memory: "Loving means to construct something together and to look together in the same direction." Obviously, there's something about all these attitudes — which are designed to preserve us from love's unexpected, painful aspects — that can kill love itself. The other day I was reading Foucault's *History of Sexuality*, in which he quotes a text by Saint François de Sales that is supposed, ostensibly, to put fidelity in a desirable light: "Man is like the elephant, for the male elephant never changes his female partner; he tenderly loves the female he has chosen; a huge beast, he is yet the most worthy of creatures." Thanks a lot!

F.G.: The same is true of the wolf or the eagle, both of which select a female and remain faithful to her for life. I loathe anthropomorphism. "Elephant dignity" — I ask you!

B.-H.L.: The only valid fidelity is the fidelity that never loses sight of the fact that the opposite is possible. For example, imagine a couple that remains faithful because of AIDS. How valid is that fidelity?

F.G.: Wise, but meaningless.

B.-H.L.: In the end, the only true fidelity is that of the mystics. I know that we're talking about lovers, but lovers should follow the example of the mystics, not of elephants. Because a mystic is what — a real mystic? It's a person who knows — and who never forgets for an instant — that man is fallible and prone to go astray. He knows that the potential for, the threat of, infidelity is always present within him. Of course, he is faithful. But his fidelity is a precarious and uncertain thing, and he is ever wary of losing sight of it — which makes it all the more precious. The saints are faithful and fallible, faithful because they *are* fallible. And there is obviously something very beautiful about that kind of fidelity.

F.G.: Yes, very beautiful. As soon as you remove love, there are some remarkable kinds of fidelity. In friendship, for example. By the way, do you believe in friendship between a man and a woman?

B.-H.L.: No . . . No, not really.

F.G.: I do. Afterward. After they've satisfied whatever desire they may have felt for each other. When there's
nothing erotic to interfere. Then, when they truly
know each other well and if there's been no unforgivable pain . . .

B.-H.L.: There's always some unforgivable pain.

F.G.: I must be able to forgive more readily than you are.

B.-H.L.: It's emotional conditioning: I always think more of
the pain I'm causing than of the pain someone is causing me.

F.G.: Bernard, you're a saint.

B.-H.L.: No, but I may be a great sinner.

F.G.: Well, when it comes down to it, you're right. I've been
caused pain, and I've caused pain, great pain. But I
never think about it.

B.-H.L.: I think about it all the time.

F.G.: Still, between former lovers it's possible to have a delightful relationship and experience lifelong fidelity in
friendship.

B.-H.L.: I wouldn't call it "friendship."

F.G.: Why not?

B.-H.L.: It's so complicated . . . so very ambiguous. Fidelity,
yes, of course; the women you've loved, yes, I think
that you remain faithful to them, in a way. But I
wouldn't call that "friendship."

F.G.: And yet . . .

B.-H.L.: How can I express it? You become strangers so
quickly, unrecognizable to each other. That's something that's always struck me: the speed with which

women from whom you've parted become strangers. Indeed, it presents a real challenge — an intellectual challenge more than an emotional one, a sentimental one. Trying to recapture, beneath the older face, the harder — or perhaps softer — expression, the imperceptible change in the voice, the evident detachment — which you quickly realize is in no way put on — this other way of moving, of dressing — trying to recapture, buried beneath all those things, the signs of some long-gone presence . . .

F.G.: I was once brought up short by something Gilles Deleuze wrote on this subject: "You will never make a friend of a woman," he wrote, "for friendship is the realization of the possible exterior world that can be offered you by another male, and only another male. And it is utopian, if not painful, to see a woman trying to express that exterior world." Obviously, for him woman represents a useless mind, a luxury . . .

B.-H.L.: I didn't know that quotation. It's weird. Where does it come from?

F.G.: Some article, "A Description of Woman," something like that. I don't have the reference here, but I'll find it. Philosophers! In the old days they used to talk about women with such amused condescension — not all of them, not Diderot, but the majority. And now they've become extraordinarily aggressive, as though they felt affronted by these "new women," the ones you deny exist. But that's another question. Are we seeing each other tomorrow?

B.-H.L.: I don't feel insulted. Truly not. Although I'm not convinced — I'll say it once more — of the existence of these "new women." But you're right, that is another question.

F.G.: To which we keep returning . . .

B.-H.L.: That's true. But we've said all there is to say about that, haven't we?

F.G.: I don't know about "all."

B.-H.L.: Working women, I agree. Sexual equality, of course. A change in attitudes, in behavior, I go along with that. But as for the rest, which means for the basics — amorous comportment, eroticism, dreams, fantasies — I obviously can't be inside a woman's head, but if I had to put money on it, once again, here's what I think: There's been no real basic mutation between you and Diderot's mistress, Sophie Volland, between the "free" woman of the eighteenth century and the woman of today.

F.G.: Between Sophie Volland and me there was the nineteenth century, which was terrifying, crushing for women in every respect, a lead coffin! Eighteenth-century women are much closer to us than nineteenth-century women. If only because no one questioned their intelligence and because they deployed it with such charm! But I certainly wouldn't use the word "mutation." There's been change, there are changes that have necessarily affected what you call "the basics." There's the change brought about by education, such a recent thing, something women were refused for so long. There's . . . there's . . . there's . . . There's now a biological woman. Today, no one can say flatly that anything has changed in feminine eroticism, in female dreams or fantasies, but there has certainly been a change in behavior. If I were you, I'd hold on to my money.

8

On the Immutability of Sexual Difference

B.-H.L.: Didn't you want to talk about this question of the new woman, the new man, and so on?

F.G.: I don't know; it's up to you.

B.-H.L.: Well, first, I think we've exhausted the subject, and, secondly, I'm the wrong person to talk about it with.

F.G.: Because?

B.-H.L.: Because even if you're right, even if there has been this "in-depth revolution," even if women and men, and the relations between them, have changed, I'd probably be the last person to know about it. I grew up with it, it was going on at the same time I was becoming aware of women. The first women I loved were the children of that event.

F.G.: I see no reason to dwell on it. Although there *is* a certain male "uneasiness" about women's liberation that I would have liked to explore. In particular the odd situation fathers find themselves in today. That's a major subject. But if you don't feel that it —

B.-H.L.: Oh, we can talk about fathers.

F.G.: It's a problem that causes concern on two counts. First, the father image has become blurred ever since the father has ceased to be the "bread winner," the sole person to bring money into the household. What is a father for? — especially when he works hard and isn't at home much. Whereas the mother, even if she also works hard, is present in every life situation that matters for the child. That's the first count. Daughters of such fathers may ask themselves: "What is a man for?"

B.-H.L.: Daughters or sons. As you know, such was the case with Aragon.

F.G.: With Aragon it was even more complicated.

B.-H.L.: Complicated, and a bit crazy. A mother who passed him off as her brother . . .

F.G.: Let's say that it had an effect on him.

B.-H.L.: Or consider the case of Malraux, or of Sartre, or of Camus — it's odd, isn't it, all those fatherless writers who experienced problems with their familial relationships.

F.G.: A dead father is quite different from an absent or separated father. Death can provide a very strong image, one to be confronted, one to be dealt with.

B.-H.L.: So many dramas of paternal failure, neglect,
shortcomings. In a certain way, literature seems to
tell us about little else. And not only tells about it —
the subject may even be literature's true source, its
prime inspiration. What is a writer, after all? He's
someone who replays, reinvents his origins. He's
someone who inscribes himself in literature and then
rewrites it. The father, and his reinvention. Law and
its transgression.

F.G.: It would be a fine subject for a thesis, but not mine. I
was talking about those children deprived of a father
who is still alive somewhere, and of fathers deprived
of their children. There are more than two million
"broken homes," more than six hundred thousand
children who never see their father. The women aren't
always responsible for this, but they are to a large degree. According to the stereotype of the modern
woman, with which they identify, they consider themselves liberated mothers but good mothers. In other
words, they don't abandon their children. And since
they usually get custody in the divorce, it's the father
who's got rid of. When the couple is unmarried, which
is common — in the past twenty years the number of
unwed fathers has increased tenfold — the question of
his keeping the children doesn't even come up if the
woman is against it. She has all the rights. In other
words, if a man wants to succeed at being a full-time
father, he has to see to it that he keeps the mother

happy. The sociologist Evelyne Sullerot has called it the strategy of the weak, one that women have been employing for decades. But men aren't used to doing it, and they employ it with varying degrees of success.

B.-H.L.: I'm unaware of it.

F.G.: There's a lot that could be said on the subject, but I won't go on.

B.-H.L.: No, no; it's important. I say, "I'm unaware of it," but I know that it's important.

F.G.: Women bear a great responsibility for this deterioration of the male image and for taking over control of the children.

B.-H.L.: With me, the experience has been the other way around. The "new fathers" who emerged post–May 1968, who were helped — or forced — by circumstances to "take control" of their children and to combine, re-create, reinvent their roles — father, mother, big brother, role model, confidant . . . But why talk about that? The whole thing was so mixed up with all the other things that were going on.

F.G.: One doesn't preclude the other.

B.-H.L.: I say "new fathers," I mention "May 1968," and right away I wonder: What was really so new about it? Wasn't it really just the same old emotional mishmash?

F.G.: It was, but there was a difference, even if one was just as torn up about it. If a woman decides to allow her husband to keep a child because she thinks it would be better for it, she's regarded as a bad mother and made to feel guilty.

B.-H.L.: That's true.

F.G.: The whole thing isn't all that simple. But it's a very serious matter, very serious, it's a whole subject to itself, the fate children are suffering because of the way the couple has changed, and particularly the way women have changed. Self-concern, which is the major feature of our era — call it individualism if you like — how can that be adapted to include the love of children, who are so demanding, who require so much daily sacrifice? An immense problem. But I'm really straying from the point. Excuse me.

B.-H.L.: I'm going to back up a little. This thing about "uneasiness." Why did you speak of "uneasiness," why are you always saying that men are "uneasy." You say, "Women have become emancipated." All right. But even if you're right, even if we are witnessing the emergence of a new, freer, truer, more equal, more whatever-you-like woman, I don't see why that should be a disaster for men. Indeed, it should be the opposite, it should be very good news.

F.G.: I agree, for those men who truly like women. For that matter, such men often say so and show it. The days of lovebirds or appealing servant girls are over; men are now faced with women who are much more interesting to seduce, to hold on to, women of whom they can be proud, with whom, in any event, they feel "involved."

B.-H.L.: Right.

F.G.: But, as we've agreed, the man who likes women is not in the majority.

B.-H.L.: As Baudelaire said, "The love of intelligent women is a pederastic pleasure." It's the only one of his witticisms I find stupid, even a little vulgar.

F.G.: So many men have lost confidence in themselves, so many have been put off balance by the independence financial autonomy has created for women. So many are quite simply afraid of women, they panic the minute they think they've detected some superior trait in a woman. Such men feel their very virility is being threatened, and that can make them very nasty. They're the worst kind of misogynists.

B.-H.L.: I agree. Except that I don't understand why you keep bringing financial autonomy into it.

F.G.: Because that's the key to the whole thing! To independence, at any rate.

B.-H.L.: I'm really going to shock you, but I don't think that money really suits women.

F.G.: Well, the lack of it certainly doesn't!

B.-H.L.: I'd have a hard time loving a female banker. Or a businesswoman.

F.G.: There's a big difference between a female banker and a woman who doesn't need to rely on someone else to pay her rent!

B.-H.L.: When I'm having lunch with a woman, I find the very thought of her picking up the check incongruous.

And as for splitting it . . . let's not even talk about that. The thought of lunching together "like pals," splitting the check . . .

F.G.: That's something else. A woman can have a good bank balance and still be tactful.

B.-H.L.: A man can be poor *and* gallant.

F.G.: But we're talking about money, Bernard — not a fortune, just the money one earns, the money one lives on more or less comfortably. That money represents power, power over one's own life, or at any rate over one's own expenses, one's whims. It's not having to feel guilty every time you want to be a little extravagant. And there's a lot that could be said about female guilt with regard to money, even when they've earned it themselves. However . . . This power of having it available and controlling it, that's what some men can't stand seeing get away from them.

B.-H.L.: I don't agree. I don't think that at all. What are you trying to say, that men would be upset at seeing their wives earn money and use that money to pay for some of their own amusements? What an idea! What a weird notion! None of the men I know, none of my friends, thinks that way.

F.G.: It's not a question of "amusements," it's a question of in-de-pen-dence.

B.-H.L.: Well, let's get things perfectly straight then. You can have a wife who has a profession, who earns money, and, to begin with, you can have no desire at all to know what she does with it, and, secondly, the notion that it might enable her to liberate herself, go off on her own, will never enter your head.

F.G.: Because you're sure of yourself.

B.-H.L.: Where I'm old-fashioned is that I find it very strange even to talk about it. There are couples who draw up "budgets," who "plan" their expenditures. There are even some who "share" them. Like going halves on the rent, or one will pay for the winter vacation and the other for the summer. Personally, I prefer doing things differently and leaving such questions more flexible. You may find that a bit hypocritical, and you'd be right. You can say that if I were a factory worker and the women in my life were salesgirls in some department store, I might think differently — and you'd be right again. Although I'm not so sure . . . Money, worry about money, the other great killer of love.

F.G.: There's no question about it. Especially the lack of it. The ideal is for each to earn enough that they never have to discuss it.

B.-H.L.: Not necessarily. No, not necessarily.

F.G.: It's funny. You're much younger than I, and I sometimes have the impression I'm listening to my great-uncle Adolphe, a dear man, who always used to say, "No woman of my family will ever work while I'm alive."

B.-H.L.: I don't go along with that.

F.G.: No, of course not. I just mean that you're something of
    a throwback.

B.-H.L.: When I was in my teens, I was fascinated by two
    "types" of women. The first was the upper-class
    woman — more precisely, the upper-class wife. You
    know . . . rich men's wives, the wives of important
    men, women who are protected by their influential
    and thoughtful husbands from ever having even to
    think about money or its uses. Charming women,
    often beautiful. They are provided the most exquisite,
    gilded lives imaginable, but then you look at them
    very carefully and you see something vacant in their
    eyes, some veiled melancholy. You see the boredom
    that surrounds them, their sudden irresolution, the
    way they can be upset if someone at a dinner party
    happens to ask them — a vacuous question, I admit,
    but one that gets asked all the same — what they do
    with their time.

F.G.: They're bored to death.

B.-H.L.: Women like that are supposed to be happy, spoiled.
    But you can sense that inside them something has bro-
    ken. Their curiosity, their interest in the world has dried
    up. They become vague, sometimes a bit unbalanced,
    and that condition can really surface when they turn
    fifty and their husband the company director ups and
    leaves them. It was a pleasure to seduce women like
    that. Because it was both easy (they were so bored!) and
    terribly difficult (so few things were capable of pene-

trating the wall of their indifference!) — and also because they usually turned out to be very gentle, very considerate lovers. However, at the same time I used to sense the disastrous side of their lives, the disorder, the profound unhappiness. They were alive and they were insulated from life. They lived high on the social ladder and apart from society. They were detached, disattached. They were women around whom a kind of vacuum had been created.

F.G.: Such women still exist. They're a bit sad. You never know what to say to them.

B.-H.L.: Yes. They're strange creatures. I say that they were gentle and considerate lovers, and that's true. In a way, that's all they had to do. But now that I think of it, there was also such colossal selfishness, such calculated caution, such "One mustn't miss," above everything else, one's vacation at Megève, somebody's New Year's party, even those deadly dull dinners where people ask you what you do but that are still such a necessary and essential part of one's life. Women like that have their moments of daring, but they're only half daring, a quarter daring, they take carefully thought out, calculated steps where there's never any question of putting anything "essential" at risk. From that point of view things have regressed since the last century. In those days that kind of woman really lost her head. Emma Bovary is the very personification of a woman in the process of losing her head — and she's not an isolated example. Whereas today's Emmas all tend not to go any farther than a weekend at the family place in Normandy, with — if possible — the connivance of the complacent servants. What's happened? What's changed? I don't know.

F.G.: Perhaps it's merely that nobody *asks* them to lose their heads any more? That such excessive behavior would only make people regard them with dismay and surprise? And they know it?

B.-H.L.: That's a nice answer. But I don't think it's correct. What's wrong with having a little fling? And if it makes your husband just doubtful or suspicious enough to reawaken his interest, so much the better. But you'd better not expect such women to act on their emotions and really burn their bridges. No, I can promise you . . .

F.G.: So your upper-class women are actually very middle-class.

B.-H.L.: For once, I'm going to be the one to take the historical and sociological point of view. I think that the real change has been divorce. In the old days there was no divorce. A woman with adultery on her mind could let herself go, and she could let herself go quite far. Should she be found out, the worst that would happen would be that she would have to come to a kind of "gentleman's agreement," which was very prevalent, at least to the end of the Belle Epoque, in good Parisian society. You find situations like that in Balzac, where a character like Maxime de Trailles carries on affairs in several novels with a variety of married women at various levels of society. There are others. There's the hero of *No Tomorrow*, Vivant Denon's little-known but wonderful novel. These are deceived husbands, of course, but they accommodate themselves to their role and, willy-nilly, accept the wife's lover. Today, Maxime de Trailles would break things off. At once. And since his wife knows this, she takes every possible precaution to keep her secret from getting out, she keeps a cool head, she cur̃bs her passion a bit and refuses to commit any kind of folly. That, believe me, is what the modern Bovary is like.

F.G.: I think you're right. Today's Emma Bovarys — because they still exist, and not only in the upper classes — rarely risk losing their comforts. And that includes a husband. Which means, of course, that they aren't true Bovarys. For Emma, the husband was the very element she was rejecting with the most horror. She dreamed of rising in society. But all the same, once in a while some woman in love will throw everything over and cause a huge ruckus and the whole town knows about it. We both know women like that. However, if I understand you correctly, you think that easy divorce has served to strengthen the bonds of the adulterous couple? That's original, but it's probably correct.

B.-H.L.: Easy divorce has made people — women in particular — more discreet. More expert in the art of lying. More secretive. Adultery viewed as a fine art . . .

F.G.: Probably . . . But when passion knocks, discretion often flies out the window. I don't know whether one would call it a good thing or a bad thing, but it seems to me that great passions are tending to become more and more rare. Or perhaps it's just that they're no longer artificially nourished on dreams and popular novels like they used to be, on some vague notion that once in your life you must experience a great passion. The "model" love affair, the one you find in movies, for example, has changed a great deal. We've already mentioned Rougemont, who inveighed against the Occidental notion of ideal passion. What he was saying, in short, was that such passions weren't acted out before us, if people didn't know that such passions *could* exist, they'd never feel them. That's wishful thinking. But I do think that such depictions are less widespread than they used to be. Indeed, what *is* the "model" love affair today, the one that young people, or people who are not so young, all cling to? I don't know, do you?

B.-H.L.: No, I don't. It's hard to know. I would say, instinctively, that here again things haven't changed all that much and that people still have the same attraction — ambiguous but strong — to the classic idea of passion. Something like: "To be in love is to be no longer quite yourself, it's to lose yourself, to turn into someone else, possibly even to become subjected to someone else, and therefore it's a frightening adventure, it's one of the worst things that can befall a man or a woman, but all the same, in the final analysis, it's one of the rare adventures, the spice of life, it's what makes life worth living."

F.G.: I think you're right. The "grand passion" has retained its prestige, its slightly wicked attraction. It may be hell, but one still longs to get a bit singed.

B.-H.L.: That's one way of putting it.

F.G.: But we're getting off the subjec⸱ We were talking about women and money. You were saying that it was your opinion that there were two fairly stereotypical types.

B.-H.L.: Right.

F.G.: You have the bourgeois woman, and we've dealt with her. And then there's the other. What type is she?

B.-H.L.: Let's call her the "driving" woman. The woman who takes control, who takes charge of her life. The dynamic woman. The woman of power, the career woman. The woman you see in the morning, up at dawn, having business breakfasts in important hotel restaurants. The cigar-smoking woman. The woman who plays golf. In a word, the masculine woman who's borrowed all of the male's least likable traits. I know that in a way it represents some kind of "progress," and I also know that once more you're going to tell me I remind you of your uncle Adolphe.

But in my opinion that is not the most flattering role
for an attractive woman. I'm always somewhat un-
comfortable when I see them like that, up too early,
made-up too quickly, their hair not quite right, their
lipstick a bit crooked, talking business with some TV
or bank executive. Baudelaire's condemnation of
George Sand's masculine side was awful and severe.
I'll just say that I find this second type just as pitiful, to
say the least, as the out-of-touch bourgeois woman.

F.G.: Smoking cigars — disgusting! And at breakfast! You
can't really meet very many women like that! As for
golf: why not? But you paint a very odd portrait. Ac-
tive women are generally very well turned out.
Rushed, but still well groomed, and if one morning
they happen not to be, what does that indicate? Only
that on that particular morning their main concern
was not to give pleasure, and a woman who doesn't
want to give pleasure — well, she *must* be ugly! See
how you are? You're not only convinced that men are
stronger, more intelligent, more courageous, more creative, more logical — in short, superior! — but you
think that women are wearing themselves out imitat-
ing them and that in addition they're losing their
much-vaunted femininity by doing so. As if femininity were something you left behind on your chair. Oh,
you make me sad! Baudelaire also said that woman
was a bag of pus . . . you really pick your sources well.
Of course the only ones he liked were whores, and
preferably syphilitic to boot.

B.-H.L.: Poor Baudelaire . . . let's leave him out of it, shall we?

F.G.: I'm not the one who brought him up.

B.-H.L.: True.

F.G.: Fine.

B.-H.L.: That being said, where whores are concerned, was he really all that wrong? I've known some who were charming.

F.G.: That's not what we're talking about.

B.-H.L.: What am I saying, in the end? Certainly not — and you're well aware — that men are "more intelligent, more courageous, more creative, more logical." Certainly not that female writers, female journalists, female artists, female philosophers, are less talented or less interesting than their male counterparts. But yes: a certain type of power, the trappings of power, don't coincide with my idea of how women fit into the world.

F.G.: Now we've come to the real question: how women fit into the world, how they go together with power. You know Pierre Bourdieu's remark that "being a man is to be placed in a position that involves power." Then you can say, contrariwise, that to be a woman has long meant being put in a position involving subjection, even obedient submission.

B.-H.L.: Wait a minute! That's something else. I hope you're not going to accuse me of being in favor of female subservience!

F.G.: Things have changed in the past twenty years, the

system has broken down, women have shaken things up — indeed, often with the help of some men, the more solid, the more adult men, men who don't feel their virility is being threatened because some powers are passing into female hands.

B.-H.L.: There you are.

F.G.: Of course other men have suffered, are suffering, thrown off balance by dynamic, victorious women. Fortunately they are less numerous in France than elsewhere, in the United States especially, where they're really unhappy. In France, relations between men and women are and remain the best in the world, even if it isn't always paradise.

B.-H.L.: There, we're in agreement, and for the nth time. And I was the first to rejoice when, for example, we had our first female prime minister. You remember the off-color jokes that made the rounds at the time, the stories some people told, the veiled references others made. You remember, the very first day, the man who was snickering about Mitterrand's "Pompadour." The whole thing was disgusting. And — it cannot be denied — you had to speak out against it.

F.G.: I'm happy to hear you say so.

B.-H.L.: Simply put, this is my position: Once again, bravo to those women who've gained power and, most importantly, have learned to enjoy it. Personally, power doesn't excite me. I don't find it desirable, and thus, for me, it's not that aspect of them that makes such women desirable.

F.G.: You went farther than that a while ago. You were talking about messy lipstick and I don't know what . . .

B.-H.L.: Yes. I don't think that suits them. There are probably men for whom the fact that a woman is a business executive only adds to her charm. With me, it's just the opposite. I prefer to forget about it and to see women like that in other settings, at other times of the day than when they're engaged in carrying out their business functions.

F.G.: Who's stopping you? There's the business relationship and there are the others, fortunately.

B.-H.L.: And another thing. This thing about badly coiffed, badly made up women — and I'm going to surprise you again — it's quite understandable. It's all part of the same basic injustice, the original scandal. A man can get by with being sloppily dressed, unshaven.

F.G.: No!

B.-H.L.: A pretty woman with tired eyes, a bad complexion — that's always a bit sad.

F.G.: I still maintain that busy women are usually well groomed and that that evening you'll find the same woman who's perhaps been a bit careless earlier is now glamorous, transformed. Women are like chameleons. No, that's not the question. I quite understand the problem some men have, brought up in a certain mold, at having to work under a woman's authority.

B.-H.L.: I don't. On the other hand, I don't see myself going to bed with such women.

F.G.: There's a whole male system that's breaking down.

You can't blame the men. It will take time for mental
patterns to change, it will take generations. But why
shouldn't women have power too, why shouldn't
they exert whatever power they can? Is there some
kind of curse that has condemned them to a sub-
servient role for all eternity? You talk about the trappings of power — they're unappealing whoever holds
the power, a man or a woman. But you've got to realize that for women power is something new, that
many of them aren't yet confident with it and so they
overdo it. It's a little silly, but it's not done to be unpleasant. Here too, it will take time.

B.-H.L.: Now it's my turn to tease you. You talk about this
with incredible condescension, like someone talking
about former colonies learning to be independent.

F.G.: Condescension! Surely not! Maybe age-old experience,
the experience of a woman who's seen a lot of water
run under the bridge and a lot of women come
to grips with this question of power. But condescension . . . that's not part of my nature.

B.-H.L.: Of course it is — the condescension of a woman
who's been a success at it. Because it's a fact that
you're one of those rare women who've managed to
make power and attractiveness compatible.

F.G.: Have I? I don't know. Looking back, I don't feel that
the combination was all that difficult.

B.-H.L.: So I'm thinking, seeing you function, about the
same question. Very seriously now, it's my turn to ask

you: Françoise, do you really like women? Do you
enjoy their company as much as you think you do?

F.G.: It all depends on the women, what they're interested
in. Sometimes, yes, I have nothing to say to them — although if they're attractive I always take pleasure in
looking at them.

B.-H.L.: You see: condescension.

F.G.: Not at all. I have a group of very dear woman friends.
Women who are attractive, and with whom I also have
a great many interests in common. We chatter away
like magpies. One of them is a journalist on an important weekly magazine. When her husband sees us together, he always says: "Don't disturb the women,
they're talking politics."

B.-H.L.: Let's try to get to the bottom of it. Listening to you
makes me wonder why I find my poor female com-
pany executive so undesirable — even (and I suppose
this goes without saying) if she is, as you claim, im-
peccably well groomed and the rest of it.

F.G.: That's for you to tell me. Maybe it's because of a kind
of self-assurance, an authority she derives from her
job. It's a commonplace to say that men like the appearance of fragility in a woman because it allows
them to cherish the illusion of their own strength. And
I grant you that your cigar-smoking executive women
are hardly little china shepherdesses in need of protec-
tion. But there may be something else.

B.-H.L.: There's always something veiled, concealed, in

what makes a woman attractive — we were saying
this the other day. And it's that aspect of her that you
can't put your finger on that's erotic. Well, when it
comes to one of these women whose taste for power
has taken precedence over their other passions, I wonder if we're not dealing with a very simple feeling,
namely, that that thing you can't put your finger on,
that thing that makes women such foreign, distant,
unattainable creatures, is, first of all, something that
we men have known all about for some time and, secondly, that we know that, in the end, it's not really all
that important.

F.G.: It's a mistake to think that the taste for power takes
precedence over other passions. Oh, with some women,
perhaps, whose struggles have been particularly difficult. But they're a small minority, and what's more,
they're rarely very young women. The "woman in
power" is at least forty years old, often older, and at
that age, yes, she may give priority to that passion. But
that's not the kind of woman who interests you. However, I'm willing to admit that power, a power, drains
more attractiveness out of the woman who exercises it
than it adds to her. That's a fact. Is it for the reason
you've cited? Maybe. But I think that it's a little more
complicated and that, above all, power reactivates the
image of the bad mother, the all-powerful mother.

B.-H.L.: The mother image . . . Men aren't against the
mother image. Or if they are against it, it's more that

they're against . . . No, I'm going to stick to it: The only thing they're interested in — that we're all interested in, I feel — is the difference between the sexes. But that's what we're supposed to be talking about tomorrow, isn't it?

F.G.: Well, we can say a few words about it now if you like.

B.-H.L.: Fine.

F.G.: Of course there's a difference between the sexes, and there always will be. Fortunately.

B.-H.L.: So you reject the feminist notion that there's an acquired, inherited, cultural difference?

F.G.: You have to make a distinction between the acquired characteristics, which are in a way superimposed, and the innate characteristics.

B.-H.L.: Where do you draw the line? How can you tell the difference?

F.G.: The prototype of the weak women who faints at the sight of a mouse, and the prototype of the strong man, the Marlboro Man, who's afraid of nothing, are equally artificial, even if generations of men and women have introjected it. Where women are concerned, they have been gradually rejecting such prototypes. Men no longer know quite where they are. They're wavering between the strong man and whatever a new man may turn out to be.

B.-H.L.: Oh? New?

F.G.: The one whose arrival Elisabeth Badinter, perhaps optimistically, has predicted, the man who will be reconciled with his sublimated feminine components, just as women today are accepting their masculine components. I believe in the male traits — self-control, the will to excel, the taste for risk and challenge, just as I believe in female traits — compassion, tenderness, sensitivity. But as a matter of fact neither of the sexes has a monopoly on any of those traits; they belong to humanity and should all temper each other.

B.-H.L.: The only real question is: Do you believe that there's a male identity and a female identity and that the two identities are basically separate? I believe that. It's been that way since the dawn of time. It will go on being that way until the twilight of time. Unless there's some revolution, I mean a mutation of the human species, the end of our world, the beginning of a new one.

F.G.: Do you really believe that there is any similarity between the warrior of the Middle Ages and today's office worker? Do you really believe that nothing has happened in the meantime, that men — and women — are still basically the same as they were? I don't. There hasn't been any mutation or metamorphosis of the human species, but there has been an evolution. Starting with a change in values.

B.-H.L.: Of course. I'm not denying that there's been an evolution! I'm saying that for the first time in its history humanity is cherishing the dream of a kind of blotting out, or erasure, of the great sexual divide. You mention Elisabeth Badinter — isn't that what she's saying? Isn't she the one who's even talked about "pregnant" men? As far as I'm concerned that dream is crazy. And silly.

F.G.: I agree with you there. A science-fiction nightmare. I think she's given that up, fortunately.

B.-H.L.: I'd like to be simultaneously both more and less radical. More, because to my mind they're not only "traits," they're actual identities. In other words, they are basic, essences. In other words, again, they're real ways of looking at the world — and there is a real gap, a metaphysical abyss, between them. And I'd be less radical, because the advantage of an identity is that you can play with it, have fun with it, go beyond it or outside it.

F.G.: I can't go along with your notion of identity including bravery, for example, a trait that has been imputed to men for so long and one that no one today would dare say shouldn't be imputed to women as well. Defining the precise identity of one sex or the other is not that easy . . . But I do believe that there are two identities. And two visions of the world as well, and that there is indeed a gap between them.

B.-H.L.: Stendhal says precisely the same thing in a chapter of *De l'amour*. He speaks of the pleasure women derive from "being able in the fire of danger to vie with man's firmness," of their way of "rising above whatever fear may weaken men in that moment." And he

quotes a wonderful sentence by some historian: "The
moment when all men lose their heads is the moment
at which women assume an incontestible superiority."

F.G.: You can always count on Stendhal.

B.-H.L.: On the one hand, resist the temptation of unisexu-
ality, of the neuter, or of androgyny, which is the great
temptation of our time. On the other . . .

F.G.: Does it bother you, my dear Bernard, when I talk
about a man's female component, your female component? A woman gave birth to you, she carried you inside her for nine months, she fed you. And don't you
realize that you've been permanently marked by that?
As has every human being, however it may affect
them.

B.-H.L.: Indeed. You interrupted me. I was going to say that
what is really at stake may be, on the one hand, to reject the notion that the two sexes together make one.
On the other hand, however, once the difference has
been made, the division established, once we've got
rid of all those silly notions about our fundamental
"dual" nature, we can play with those roles, invert
them, complicate them. But careful — I view that as a
strategy of seduction. It's got nothing to do with stories about mothers or repressed femininity.

F.G.: They're all so stupid, those stories about mothers. Do
you know what your conversation has reminded me
of? A bit of dialogue from somewhere, perhaps from
Nina Berberova's *L'Accompagnatrice*. A man asks a

young woman, "Is it too hard to be a woman?" "I think so," the girl replies."They all complain about it." And he says: "In any event, it's impossible to be a man. No one succeeds at that." And by the way, I've just realized that we haven't once mentioned young women.

B.-H.L.: That's right.

F.G.: "Wise young women, a sea league beneath their eyelids . . ." Valéry is always incredible, it's the "wise" that's beautiful.

B.-H.L.: I've never had a passion for very young women.

F.G.: But they are so mysterious. With that mixture of uncompleted childhood and heightened femininity.

B.-H.L.: Yes, but that doesn't really appeal to me. Even when I was very young, I wasn't attracted to girls who were too young.

F.G.: To tell the truth, I'm not sure I know today's young women. I know the boys, but not the girls.

B.-H.L.: There's something in their amorous behavior that has always bothered me somehow. It's that touch of childhood, as you said. That transparency. That confidence. And, in the end, the absence of guile . . .

F.G.: Don't be so sure.

B.-H.L.: Maybe. But still, that's often what men find attractive about very young girls, that sort of innocence, an *image* of innocence. Well, I guess I'm not fascinated by innocence.

F.G.: I'm very aware of the physical grace of young girls.

That gesture they all make these days, for example, of tucking a strand of hair behind their ears with their finger. It's so pretty.

B.-H.L.: True, there are period gestures just as there are period expressions.

F.G.: The only thing is that young women are often fixated on strange problems . . . endless days that seem to drag by, the long, long time before the undefinable thing they're waiting for will happen.

B.-H.L.: Were you a happy young girl?

F.G.: There *are* no happy young girls.

9

On Seduction and Its Games

F.G.: In our enthusiasm we've barely touched on one delicate subject, namely, seduction.

B.-H.L.: Right.

F.G.: Of course, the first thing that comes to mind is the image of Don Juan. Don Juan's a bit meaningless nowadays, but he's still the only modern myth, the only truly mythic figure since the days of the ancient Greeks . . . along with Don Quixote. What kind of man typifies Don Juan today? How does he go about his seductions? What are his weapons?

B.-H.L.: Here again, I don't think there's been much change, in weapons, in strategy, or in anything else.

F.G.: I agree. But how would you describe today's Don Juan type?

B.-H.L.: Two basic qualities: First, he's had them all. Second: I'm going to be the last one.

F.G.: That's what the woman who's been seduced is thinking. This "I'm going to be the last one" is the great seductive illusion."I'll be able to hold on to him." But what makes Don Juan run? Why does he dash madly from woman to woman? What is he searching for? As you know, there are various interpretations. What's yours?

B.-H.L.: My interpretation? You're being funny. It's one thing if you're talking about the literary Don Juan, the Don Juan of Molière or Mozart. There's the character's damnation, his status as a rebel, his relationship with the Deity. Because you can't get away from that. Don Juan's real quarrel is with heaven. Indeed, that's what got Molière's play banned back when it was written. But if we're talking about the other, modern, present-day Don Juan, that's something else.

F.G.: The first one is more attractive, but we're living with the latter. Now I'll quote Albert Cohen, when he wonders what lies behind Don Juan's passion for seducing women although he is really chaste, with little liking for what happens in bed, which he finds monotonous, rudimentary, and only resigns himself to it because "they want it." The prime motive behind his rage to seduce, Cohen says, is the hope of failure, that someday some woman will resist him.

B.-H.L.: One thing is sure, and that is the character's dissatisfaction, his inability to find gratification. The Don

Juan complex must have this basic dissatisfaction. So we have two hypotheses: either this inability to achieve gratification is — we'll call it "pathological," for lack of a better term — or it is in the nature of things, it is telling us something about the nature of desire, the truth about desire. And what it is telling us is that desire equals emptiness, that desire is a negative quality, that desire is essentially the inability to attain, to embrace, its object. That is the other interpretation.

F.G.: Is it yours?

B.-H.L.: More or less.

F.G.: Does that mean that all men go through their Don Juan phase and that it's basically pathological, or that it's in the nature of desire, that they are all more or less fascinated by the image of this tireless seducer who gobbles women up like peanuts?

B.-H.L.: Yes. That's an inescapable part of it, since the Don Juan syndrome implies this kind of recognition of the truth of desire. Every man is tempted to be a Don Juan because every man knows that desire is never fulfilled.

F.G.: Let's try to be more precise. An actual Don Juan, in today's society . . . How does he operate? What are his motivations?

B.-H.L.: There are a lot of things. For example, there's the spectacle offered by the majority of couples — their mediocrity, their discontent. The other day I was talk-

ing about my distrust of the celibate discourse that
was so prevalent in the nineteenth century, and I
needn't say that I equally distrust the conjugal model
that became established in the same nineteenth century. When you examine that, how can you help being
tempted by fantasies, by adventure?

F.G.: I certainly don't believe that the conjugal model you
mention has given rise to libertinism. If it had, the Don
Juan syndrome would have disappeared with the arrival of what we can call the "modern" conjugal
model. But it's still prevalent, and very little different.

B.-H.L.: You're right.

F.G.: Fine. So let me ask you again: What's the reason for
this tendency, this folly? Why this fever that drives
men from woman to woman?

B.-H.L.: Is it a fever? I'm not sure. The prototype of Don
Juan — Valmont, the male protagonist of *Liaisons Dangereuses* — is quite the opposite of a feverish creature,
as you know. He's cool-headed and calculating, a
strategist, a man whose partners know — and are in-
timidated by knowing — that the prime virtue is "the
intellect."

F.G.: Laclos uses the term "principles." He writes that Valmont is a "man of principles." He even goes on to say
that that is his blackest, most unpardonable crime. Valmont would be innocent if he were merely acting in
the grip of passion. He's to be condemned because he
does nothing without having meticulously thought it
through.

B.-H.L.: Right. So you're asking me why, what is Don Juan's motive, his constant thought, his constant calculation? There is, you know, a simple explanation, namely, curiosity. A while ago you mentioned "monotony." And it's true — Cohen is right — there's nothing more monotonous than the scenario of a seduction. But remember, there's a lot more to it than that! There's the result! You'll excuse me if I speak very frankly, but I do not at all believe that the result of seduction is in any way monotonous — not at all!

F.G.: You don't?

B.-H.L.: On the contrary, it couldn't be more diverse, more varied. No two women in the world — or no two men, I imagine —are alike when it comes to the actual sex act. Each time it's like breaking a new code . . . there are new emotions, the caresses are imperceptibly different and therefore incredibly moving . . . How could anyone be so misled as to say that eroticism is the realm of uniformity, of sameness? Your Don Juan is a person who is curious about such things, and his curiosity is unquenchable — because reality itself is infinitely diverse, differentiated. Discovering a woman's *other* body, her *other* voice, her *other* gestures — what an adventure!

F.G.: So let me ask the question another way. At a time when practically no one is fanatically virtuous, when there are no more supposedly impregnable fortresses, isn't it astonishing that there should still be any pleasure in conquering them? You need someone who's all right, who's passable physically, but you don't need talent or cleverness.

B.-H.L.: As for a passable physique, you know what Stendhal said: "Beauty gives you a two-week advantage."

F.G.: Was it Stendhal? I'd have thought Talleyrand . . . but it's not important.

B.-H.L.: In any case, it's saying that beauty, physical charm, presence, play a very small role.

F.G.: So what does play a role then — just a bit of the old know-how that every ladies' man possesses?

B.-H.L.: I don't really know either. I know that that's what men say. They say it among themselves, they even say it in public. To hear them talk, all women are there for the taking, every woman is available. Fine. I may be going to disappoint you, but it's my impression that men like that brag a lot but that it's mostly talk, and that things are really just a tad more complicated.

F.G.: Because?

B.-H.L.: On the one hand, of course, there are many women who are unhappy in love, who find that they're ignored most of the time, and as long as you follow the rules, bring the appropriate machinery into play, they are often more available than they may seem at first. But careful — you need to know the rules, you need to have the wherewithal, you need that machinery. And only idiots — or braggarts — think that most women are just waiting for the opportunity to fall into their nets. In other words, I don't go along with the "bit of the old know-how every ladies' man possesses."

F.G.: So, a *lot* of "know-how." But once again: What are a man's weapons, his seduction strategy? Do you remember the playwright Henry Bernstein, who flourished early this century, a renowned "ladies' man"? He maintained that no woman could resist the daily gift of a floral offering. And, apparently, his tactic was successful — expensive, but effective. Have you ever tried that? There's also giving books, but that's difficult because it means you're crediting the woman with being capable of appreciating them. What else?

B.-H.L.: The best strategy — if it is a strategy — is still the one that consists in getting her to "tell you about herself." "Yes, tell me some more . . . you're so interesting, so different . . ." Yes, I've often observed that the real operators are the ones who can create the impression that there's nothing in the world more interesting than the life, the feelings, the emotions, the passions of the woman they're courting. But is that really a strategy? Don't men also talk a lot of nonsense when they discuss "strategy"?

F.G.: It can be unconscious, not deliberate. But there's no desire for conquest without strategy. Remember Valmont — we've just said that he was strategy personified.

B.-H.L.: The truth is that women go for men who desire them. There are so many faked desires, so many half-hearted desires, so many men who obviously give business, power, the fate of the world, their own fate, precedence over the pleasure of conquering a woman and then savoring their conquest! We've said that on several occasions since we began these conversations. The world is divided — and quite unevenly — between men who love women and men who only pretend to. And the women involved know that, don't they? They sense it immediately. And so quite naturally they give in to the former. Both the strategy and the means of implementing it come later.

F.G.: That's very true. And because seduction goes both ways, let me say that it's not so bad to like men and to please them. And that's not very widespread either.

B.-H.L.: Right. Can we talk about women now? About female know-how? That is, if there is a distinction and if there are two different "operations," male seduction, female seduction?

F.G.: There are many kinds of know-how. So many elements enter into seduction. First, of course, there's natural grace or, even more, the way it's used. The comedy of modesty or immodesty, the timid beauty, the confident beauty, the role played by clothing. Men today aren't in luck when it comes to articles of clothing, which aren't very flattering . . . excepting blue jeans, when they're worn by the right person. But women have never had such a wide range of seductive tools to help them display or conceal whatever they like: skirts so short that the temptation to slip your hand under them is almost irresistible, long, long legs, practically bare breasts, tight pants, tubes of material that pass for dresses and that cling to every inch of the body. Never

before has feminine clothing been more provocative —
excepting perhaps for a very brief moment under the
Directory at the beginning of the nineteenth century,
with the fashions of the empress Joséphine. And it's a
pleasure for a woman to be able to play the game of
seduction by using her way of dress. One of the sad
things about growing old is that you only dress to
cover yourself up.

B.-H.L.: Is it really a question of age? I've always been fascinated by female elegance . . . the elegance of all
women. And I think that it's still awfully seductive. But
all right — you can talk about it better than I ever could.

F.G.: And of course there's make up too. It too has a part to
play in seduction. And it's always existed. It's interesting, don't you think, that since the dawn of time, since
the time of the Egyptians, women have been wearing
makeup? It must correspond to something very deep
down.

B.-H.L.: Valéry said that the deepest you could go was skin
deep.

F.G.: Yes, but made-up skin. The skin made up, covered
with signs. The oldest civilizations had this.

B.-H.L.: I long ago admitted my boundless affection for
makeup. I find a woman without makeup almost vulgar. And I consider makeup to be the indication of an
advanced culture.

F.G.: There are some beautiful things about makeup in
Baudelaire.

B.-H.L.: Of course. In fact, it's one of the main "theoretical" texts.

F.G.: Louis Fourteenth's great fault was to demand that his mistresses be country fresh, to forbid them to wear makeup.

B.-H.L.: And woman must be given credit for "consolidating," for "deifying" beauty through makeup, for emulating statuary, in other words, for emulating some divinity, some superior being.

F.G.: Makeup as artifice . . .

B.-H.L.: As the rejection of nature . . .

F.G.: Poor George Sand! The main reproach against her was that she didn't wear makeup —

B.-H.L.: — and of therefore being close, too close, to nature, to original sin.

F.G.: That repulsive "Sand woman."

B.-H.L.: In fact, it's the notion that a body isn't "acceptable" unless it has been worked on, cultivated. There's the body as natural object, as something disgusting, and then there's the body as cultural artifact — and it's adorable.

F.G.: Back to Georges Bataille: A woman, a man, can be beautiful only to the precise degree to which artifice — in other words makeup — separates them from the animal.

B.-H.L.: So, in a word, I'm obviously in agreement with all that, in principle. We obviously can't help agreeing.

F.G.: Of course.

B.-H.L.: But there is one question, all the same, that I keep asking myself: Does makeup add meaning to a face, to the expression, or, on the contrary, does it remove meaning from it, does it impoverish it?

F.G.: I'd be inclined to say that it removes emotion.

B.-H.L.: That's what I end up thinking. But it's the opposite of what Baudelaire thought.

F.G.: But he singles out particular features. The eyes, for example, which are so important to the face. Or those blood-red mouths. And then the glittering white teeth. A brilliant smile is important.

B.-H.L.: It comes down to the same thing. It's because it singles out certain traits that makeup impoverishes, simplifies, caricatures the face. It reduces it to one note, removes its ambiguity. Or . . . It makes me feel strange to say it when I've always been so pro-Baudelaire, but I think that nowadays overelaborate makeup removes a face's ambiguity, its suggestiveness.

F.G.: And therefore its seductiveness.

B.-H.L.: Therefore its seductiveness.

F.G.: Even though you might also say that heavy makeup adds sexiness to a face.

B.-H.L.: That in itself, I wouldn't find unpleasant. But once again, I find that that kind of display is often lacking in subtlety and therefore in charm. An almost naked face has more eloquence and, therefore, more sensuality.

F.G.: Let's say that exaggerated makeup somehow freezes the face.

B.-H.L.: Take films. That was Eisenstein's theory. The more naked a face, the more chances it has of conveying signs, meanings.

F.G.: That's true. There's nothing more beautiful than the faces in *The Battleship Potemkin*. Or in Dreyer's films.

B.-H.L.: In reality, the ultimate goal is probably makeup that doesn't cover things up, makeup that simulates nature.

F.G.: The makeup that you don't notice.

B.-H.L.: And of course that's the reason I dislike nothing more than seeing a woman apply makeup in public, after dinner for example. It's too obvious. And thus too obscene. There's a scene like that in Virginia Woolf's novel *Mrs. Dalloway*.

F.G.: Yes, excepting that Virginia Woolf is commending this exhibitionistic trait. She views its daring as the essence of femininity.

B.-H.L.: That is true.

F.G.: And then there's another thing: Just as makeup can be pleasing on a young face, so too, when the freshness of the face is gone, the makeup can begin to resemble plaster. Because now what you're emphasizing is age.

B.-H.L.: There's the scene in Mann's *Death in Venice*, when Aschenbach, on the brink of death, goes to his hairdresser to get made up for the last time.

F.G.: And that very cruel scene in Proust's *The Guermantes Way* with all the overly made up women, the faces plastered with layers of powder, a woman whose face looks like it was made of stone.

B.-H.L.: Women should read Proust more.

F.G.: When one has racked up a few years, one should use a lighter hand. Just keep a few soft shadows.

B.-H.L.: The most cunning strategy . . .

F.G.: That being said, the most charming example of female strategy comes from Jean Giraudoux in his play *L'Apollon de Bellac*. Do you recall the scene where Agnès says that she loves men, their doglike eyes, their hair, their big feet, but that she also finds them intimidating, and a gentleman tells her: "Are you interested in getting them to do what you want? There's one infallible recipe. Tell them that they're handsome." "Tell them that they're handsome, intelligent, sensitive?" Agnès asks. "No. Just that they're handsome. Intelligence, feelings — that they know without any help." You can never overdo telling men that they're handsome, especially when they aren't, particularly.

B.-H.L.: That doesn't go only for men, you know. I've got Elsa Morante's novel *Aracoeli* with me. Listen to this: "Every creature on earth is offering itself. Pitiable, ingenuous, it is offering itself. I exist, here I am, with this face, this body, this smell. From Napoléon to Lenin and Stalin, from the lowest whore in the street to the Mongoloid child, from Greta Garbo to a stray dog, this is truly the sole and perpetual question every living creature is asking every other: Do you find me beautiful?"

F.G.: The most talented seductress of her day was Alma
      Mahler, who had a very personal technique: she had a
      very exalted notion of herself, and what she used to
      say to men was, "If you can please a woman like me
      you must obviously be someone out of the ordinary."
      They adored it. And she collected them by the carload.

B.-H.L.: There's a woman today who's like that. Yes, yes,
      not quite as good but similar. I'll tell you who it is
      when we've turned off the tape recorder. With seduc-
      tion, there's always a higher level to aspire to. It's part
      of the game — I was going to say "the ritual" — and
      it's a ritual that is, in principle, endless.

F.G.: It ends with the conquest — or with failure.

B.-H.L.: The game really becomes interesting when it's
      played by both parties. Indeed, that's the big difference
      between seduction and love. You can love alone, you
      can love without being loved in return. At least that's
      what you were saying, isn't it? Isn't that the great and
      terrible Proustian idea you were supporting? Well, you
      could never say that about seduction, it would be in-
      conceivable. Seduction without response, seduction
      without any return, without any duel, seduction with-
      out someone who is also seducing you, that would be
      utter nonsense.

F.G.: Are you saying that female and male seducers are each
      other's prisoners, that they feed on each other? I can
      accept that. But do you think that we're seducers —
      I'd almost say "by nature" — because we are unable to

help using our charms, testing our powers, from time to time selecting a victim — or a gaming partner, if you prefer?

B.-H.L.: There are people with seductive personalities, people whose motto could almost be, "I seduce, therefore I am," or, contrariwise, "I no longer seduce, therefore I might as well be dead, wiped out." Take Kierkegaard's seducer, Johannes Forfoereren. That's what he's saying.

F.G.: Kierkegaard was a pretty peculiar seducer, incidentally.

B.-H.L.: Valmont's opposite. Johannes has a "spiritual" side that Valmont lacked.

F.G.: All his seductive ploys are based more on aesthetics than on eroticism. Indeed, he says so. If I recall, he says: "I'm an aesthetician."

B.-H.L.: The remarkable thing about Kierkegaard's work on seduction is its concept of a seduction campaign that can only culminate in the gaining of total control over the person one desires. Other seducers engage in maneuvers, they lay siege to the woman they love, they batter down her defenses . . . in short, you have the whole military vocabulary we were talking about the other evening. But Kierkegaard goes much farther, he wants nothing less than to inhabit, to colonize the soul he has conquered. He wants to control her thoughts, to direct her feelings. He wants to imbue her with love, or hatred, or more love, to inspire her to further resistance. He arouses her shame. He goads her into acts that may be charming or that may be ridiculous — in other words, his true aim is not to possess her body or to become the master of her desires, it's to arrange things so that not a single movement of her soul can escape his control. Greek despots used to yield in the face of geometry; modern totalitarians will insist on getting the secrets of the soul. According to Kierkegaard, the seducer's appetite for control knows no bounds. He's the perfect tyrant. I don't recall the text very well, but this also differentiates him from Valmont.

F.G.: You haven't answered me: are we seducers by nature, by vocation?

B.-H.L.: Yes, I have answered you.

F.G.: I don't think so.

B.-H.L.: Well, I'll take an example.

F.G.: Yes?

B.-H.L.: I'll take you. May we talk about you for just a moment?

F.G.: I'm not very enthusiastic about it, but —

B.-H.L.: I remember the first time I ever met you. It was nearly twenty years ago, in an apartment in the Marais, the home of a writer who must have been a mutual friend. I had just started a newspaper called *L'Imprévu*, a daily. In the end, there were only a few issues, but at the time it was a going concern, and Michel Butel and I had just written an editorial piece about you. At the time, you must have been the Minister of something or other — the Status of Women, I imagine, or Culture . . .

F.G.: I vaguely recall that dinner party. I remember that there was a magnificent Italian tiled floor . . .

B.-H.L.: Anyhow, I'd written this piece, and I remember it ended with: "Françoise Giroud, or Halcyon Pre-Revolutionary Days." I was fairly far left in those days, and I even believed in the revolution, a bit, but before it, I wanted some halcyon days. Anyhow. The mutual friend had read the piece and had decided to bring us together. So there we both ·vere at his place, with Alex. Yes, I think Alex was there too — there were seven or eight of us, and there was Alex. Why am I telling this? Oh yes . . . "Are there seductive temperaments?" Well, you were one. You were obviously one. My memory of you from that evening is of an archetypical seductress. It was all there in the smile, the look, great attention to gestures — your own and others' — flirtatiousness, an endless fund of coquetry, and little ways of suddenly reassuring your partner, of drawing closer to him as if to deny whatever the seduction signified or might signify. I remember all that very clearly. Just as I remember thinking, when we parted, "Too flirtatious to have a real political career."

F.G.: So in the end I was saved! What an awful thing a political career is! I never wanted one because I sensed I wasn't cut out for the life of a female politician, which requires very special talents . . . and in any case, and you're right, in politics coquetry and seduction are handicaps for a woman. If she wants to succeed there, she has to be a mother figure, reassuring, but certainly not seductive. You see how Michèle Barzach was made to pay.

B.-H.L.: At the time, I used to think that there was something almost diabolical about seduction and that . . . As a matter of fact, I shouldn't say "used to think," because in a way I still do.

F.G.: Does the devil really come into it? Nothing is more difficult than to appreciate or evaluate one's own seductiveness, one's own weapons, the way one uses them. The evening you mention . . . I was already no longer a young woman, but I was loved by the man I was with, and nothing gives a person such a glow. Did I really set out to do my best to charm you? I must have, since you say so. I'm sure I must have done it spontaneously, because you were a good-looking, dynamic young man and it amused me to catch your attention. But for what purpose? For nothing. For a moment of pleasure, for the pleasure of being able, fleetingly, to charm another person. I must confess that I've enjoyed that pleasure all my life. You too, I think?

B.-H.L.: The pleasure of charming someone, of playing at seduction — what it comes down to is seduction for its own sake. Sometimes you hear a woman — or a man, although as a rule not so readily — referred to as a flirt, a "tease," and the term usually has an uncomplimentary connotation. But it's my opinion that with such women, or men, we are seeing the very essence of seduction.

F.G.: "Tease" is a vulgar term . . . All that's involved in teasing is sex. "Charming," "a charmer," those are pleasant words that evoke much more subtle forms of behavior. Offering oneself *and* holding back. Giving in *and* remaining aloof. An odd mix of playfulness and reticence.

B.-H.L.: It's another kind of desire, another game — and not necessarily an erotic one. You were asking if I enjoyed this pastime, this game of charming someone. Obviously, true seducers enjoy it. They can enjoy eroticism and at the same time they can enjoy this kind of pretending, without the two things necessarily having anything to do with each other.

F.G.: Is there a type of man or woman who arouses this desire and just plays at seduction? Or do the real charmers go into action indiscriminately, simply to see if their charm will "work"?

B.-H.L.: I'll repeat what I was saying before: Love requires an object, no matter what it is. It alights upon a "love object" without needing any "objective" reason for doing so. It's an adventure, in other words, that can be solitary. But seduction is a game that requires two players, and it can only be played with the proper partners. What makes those partners choose each other? A certain kind of fantasy . . . a certain fondness for the game . . . a knack, a real talent for enacting the rituals of seduction . . . Seductive men, and women, can always recognize each other.

F.G.: One more question: Is a man capable of being interested for more than five minutes in a woman who is lacking in seduction? You know Jules Renard's harsh judgment: "Do what you will, up until a certain age" — and I don't know what that is — "one experiences no pleasure in conversing with a woman who could not possibly become one's mistress." It reeks of the nineteenth century. Female conversation. But would you say that that still holds true?

B.-H.L.: I'd certainly say that I have a great deal of difficulty in being interested for more than five minutes in anyone, man or woman, who lacks seduction.

F.G.: Jules Renard isn't talking about some vague, generalized, random seductiveness, about mental or amicable seduction. He says "a woman who could not become one's mistress." You know how that would be expressed today.

B.-H.L.: I think I've already gone into that. It's ugly and vulgar, it's all those things. But it's true that I do not believe in friendship between men and women, and that when that touch of ambiguity is lacking, the relationship seems to me to be — what word do I want? — futile, sterile, useless. Let me defend myself by saying — and here too I'm repeating myself — that I can imagine feeling a very keen desire for a woman who is not beautiful.

F.G.: We've overlooked one highly ambiguous situation, that of a man determined to seduce a woman because she is the companion of a more powerful man whose shoes he wants to fill.

B.-H.L.: That's not all that ambiguous, nor all that unusual.

F.G.: It isn't?

B.-H.L.: It illustrates that theory — I think we've already talked about it — of mimetic, triangular desire. If that's the desire, if that's the form it takes, it's almost inevitable that some third person will come into it. I remember publishing an article a few years ago entitled "Lovemaking Is Always a Threesome," which shocked a few people. But it was so obvious! And whether the third person is the more powerful man or a woman who fascinates the woman is only a minor variation in the overall, immutable structure.

F.G.: And the love object? Is it picked out according to a fixed type? In other words, does a person have a "female type" or "male type" that instantly strikes a chord? Everyone knows Swann's famous remark at the end of Proust's *Swann in Love*: "To think that I've wasted years of my life, that I've longed to die, that I've experienced my greatest love, for a woman who didn't appeal to me, who wasn't even my type!" That's rather unusual, it seems to me.

B.-H.L.: Whereas at the very end of the whole novel, Odette, now an old woman, says exactly the opposite:

"Poor Charles, how intelligent he was, how fascinating, just the type of man I liked."

F.G.: But Odette never loved Swann.

B.-H.L.: As you said, it's unusual. I would also remind you of the first sentence of Aragon's novel *Aurélien*: "The first time I saw Bérénice I thought her downright ugly."

F.G.: An ugly woman can be desirable, we've already talked about that.

B.-H.L.: What we're saying, and Proust, and Aragon, is that desire is always improbable. People think that they have a type, they seek it out, they wait for it, they are alert to all the signals of imminent passion, in themselves and in their surroundings. They tell themselves, "For my entire life, with infinitesimal variations, I'm going to want a predetermined type," and then no, that's not what happens. Desire raises its head, yes, but in an unexpected place, in the opposite direction, as it were.

F.G.: Has that happened to you? In other words, have you been faithful to a female type or have you been eclectic?

B.-H.L.: I'd have a hard time telling you what the women I've loved have in common. A physical type? Not at all. A view of the world? Even less. Was there something in me, always the same thing, that they all appealed to? Not that either — truly not. It was always different, multifaceted — until I met the woman with whom I'm now living, whom I love as I haven't loved any other, but another woman about whom I first thought, "She's obviously not my type."

F.G.: And what is your type?

B.-H.L.: What's yours? Do you have a type, do you not have a type? Are you like Swann or unlike Swann?

F.G.: It's more complicated. First, there's the body, the physical aspect, to which I'm probably excessively sensitive. There are physical types that can be seductive to some, that are very attractive, but which completely turn me off. I shrink away from them. And then, and this goes more deeply, there's something that attracts me, something that all the men I've been in love with seem to create, and that's the psychological posture I come to adopt in their presence. Stendhal says that the first thing one loves in a man is a physiognomy that simultaneously reveals something to be respected and something to be pitied. I find that both subtle and true, at least where I'm concerned. It doesn't precisely define a type of man, but a constant.

B.-H.L.: In fact, Proust says two things. The first I find only mildly interesting: The women who aren't your "type" always turn up unexpectedly, your defenses are down, and so they become a part of your life, they gently take it over and eventually they manage to make you love them. But he also has this second theory, which I find far more true: I don't think she's my type, I don't think we're attuned to each other, whereas in reality she *is* your type, profoundly so, but so profoundly that it was almost impossible to tell at first glance — "Does her resemblance to a Botticelli have something to do with the puzzle of my love for Odette, and would I have loved her so much if she'd resembled a Rubens?" In other words, the women one loves will always turn out to be our type, even if that type isn't always visible to the naked eye, even if you were unaware of it before.

F.G.: Well, once again I agree with Proust. Even if life is long, even if at certain periods you may seem to stray from your "type." But you don't love with passion. Not the kind of passion that engulfs you.

B.-H.L.: It's very strange, this whole Proust thing.

F.G.: What do you mean?

B.-H.L.: It doesn't have anything to do with what we've been saying, but while you were talking, I was thinking: It's extraordinary, all the same, that everyone who ponders the question of love — not only you and me, but everyone — is constantly referring to Proust. He imagined that the crux of his novel would be the sections dealing with the Dreyfus affair, or that he would be remembered as a chronicler of the elegant Paris that held such fascination for him, or that it would be for what he wrote about painting, or literature, or criticism. But not at all — it's the part of it that has to do with love. That solitary man, a homosexual, that man whose sexual practices were fairly, shall we say "unorthodox," ended up becoming the great theoretician of the amorous relations between men and women.

F.G.: Why not? "Love is a lawless gypsy child," as Carmen says. I don't think there is such a thing as "heterosexual" or "homosexual" love, there's just something we call "love," period. Love in which one person always loves more than the other, one person is always more jealous than the other, one person is always in thrall to the other. Love in which one partner always waits by the telephone, as Roland Barthes (who also knew what he was talking about) put it. That's the relationship Proust explored as no one else ever has, and there's no reason to think it's any different in homosexual relationships.

B.-H.L.: For me, that's the great mystery. Unlike you, I think it's really very, very mysterious. On the one hand, I tend to believe that homosexuality implies a view of the world and, quite obviously, a kind of sexuality that are both "special." The other person's body, one's own body, the kind of fetishism that comes into play, resemblance, identity. For example, can you imagine a book like Gide's *Fruits of the Earth*, in which the hero wasn't a man? Isn't that a typical homosexual text? On the other hand, of course, there's Proust — whose Albertine was really Agostinelli and who still managed to write the bible of love. There's Barthes and *A Lover's Discourse*, which, as everyone knows, has no sex at all. There's Dante Gabriel Rossetti, who used young men as the models for the most beautiful women in his paintings — in short, there's this evidence of a two-way sensuality.

F.G.: There's nothing strange about the partner. But the twin body is a real problem. What goes on in the mind is different. What is purely erotic is probably different in nature, a nature that is impenetrable to anyone who isn't homosexual himself. But I'm convinced that the emotions — and such violent ones! — are the same.

B.-H.L.: In any event, for Proust that never caused a problem. It didn't bother him that Albertine was really called Albert, he wasn't surprised that when the Baron de Charlus read Musset's *La Nuit d' octobre*, the faithless beauty should have Morel's face.

F.G.: Right. Because he thought that there were two ways, as he put it, of "acceding to the truths of love." And that the difference between them was actually immaterial.

B.-H.L.: The other day a friend was telling me: It's all the same, the expectation, the jealousy, the desire and the fear, the gentleness and the violence, the more-or-less-reciprocal love, the seduction, everything . . . but with one small reservation, and that is the feeling that is so important with men who love women, namely, the dread (sometimes coupled with a secret pleasure) of seeing the person they love grow old. Homosexuals grow old together . . . I was going to say "in step." Whereas between men and women that is still, whatever people may say, the basic inequality.

F.G.: Quite the contrary, homosexuals suffer terribly from

growing old, they have face-lifts, they get implants when they start losing their hair, whatever. In that respect I don't think that your friend was right. In a more general way, when you think about it, the inequality between men and women when it comes to age is scandalous. I've always thought that when the time comes that they're no longer desirable, a time that isn't preordained and one that has been pushed back considerably, women should be able to turn into men. Instead of which . . . Do you remember the lines in Musset's *Les Caprices de Marianne*? "How old are you, Marianne? Eighteen? You have five or six years left to be loved, eight to ten to be in love yourself and the remainder to pray to God." Instead of which, with the awful way life is being prolonged, they've now got all of eternity to live like zombies.

10

On the Couple As Will and Idea

F.G.: Shall we go on for a little longer?

B.-H.L.: We've got the whole evening.

F.G.: This experience we've accumulated — I have more, but yours is broad — along love's highway (if I may wax poetic) . . . one sometimes wishes it could be useful in some way, that it could help other people to avoid making mistakes, avoid being hurt, keep them from . . . That it might even give them a "two-week advantage." But I'm afraid that, like all experiences, those having to do with love cannot be passed on. We can teach people things about life, we can learn such lessons — I certainly have — but when it comes to amorous relationships, I don't believe anything can ever be taught or learned. Do you share my feelings?

B.-H.L.: Yes, I do. I agree that nothing can be passed on. At least, very little can.

F.G.: Right.

B.-H.L.: Starting with one's own case. You spend your whole life starting over again. You make the same mistakes hundreds of times. You tell yourself, "Life has taught me a lesson . . . that's something I'll never do again," and then, of course, you do it anyway. And you keep on doing it. So, giving advice to others . . . How can anyone teach another person anything?

F.G.: I'd like you to be wrong, but unfortunately . . .

B.-H.L.: Plato has things to say about this. Happiness cannot be taught, he says — and especially happiness in love.

F.G.: Happiness, no; but there are other little things. Stendhal's advice, for example: "One must have an unimaginative spouse and take a romantic lover." Is that a useful lesson?

B.-H.L.: I wonder. If I had to give just one piece of advice, it would be more the opposite — a romantic spouse and an unimaginative lover.

F.G.: And then there's Freud: "A man who questions his own love may — or rather, will — question everything that is of less import."

B.-H.L.: That's an improvement.

F.G.: And then there's this: "I think that if a woman succeeds in standing out from the crowd, of rising above herself, she will keep on growing, and to a greater degree than a man!" Who do you think said that?

B.-H.L.: I've no idea.

F.G.: You'll never guess. The greatest misogynist of all, Schopenhauer. So we can believe him.

B.-H.L.: Or distrust him. If I were you, I'd distrust.

F.G.: Then there's Napoléon's famous remark, "The only victory in love resides in flight." Isn't that something you'd like to have hanging above your bed?

B.-H.L.: Like to or not, it's something we've all done, alas! As for giving the same advice to others . . .

F.G.: Imagine that your best friend introduces you to some unattractive, cross-eyed cripple and says, "I'm crazy about her and I'm going to marry her." If you answer, "You can't really have taken a good look at her . . . ," you'll lose him forever.

B.-H.L.: I'd never say that to him. Once again, I'm far too conscious of how arbitrarily you can single out the woman you fall in love with.

F.G.: In any event, there's nothing more mysterious than other people's love affairs. In most cases we find their choice of partner incomprehensible.

B.-H.L.: We find our own choices incomprehensible — how can other people help doing the same?

F.G.: No, I'd say that we find our own choices very obvious. It's other people who sometimes find them ridiculous.

B.-H.L.: True, we're often at a loss about other people's passions, their origins, what inspires them, their objects. This woman some man thinks is a saint, this other woman who says she loves a man when she is obviously just leading him on, venal women, women who are real professionals, the lies they tell men and that men swallow with such naïveté . . .

F.G.: Please — the lies that women tell men and the lies that men tell women . . .

B.-H.L.: Of course.

F.G.: But do we call them lies? I think it's more subtle than that. They have such consistency, such braggadocio. But it's true that you don't understand how the other person can be so blind.

B.-H.L.: You frequently wonder, "What can he possibly see in her, how is it that this otherwise intelligent, powerful man, whatever, can let himself be taken in by that ridiculous creature?"

F.G.: And how can she let herself be bamboozled by that pretentious windbag? Good question. Why do you tie yourself down to someone who everyone else considers to be ill suited to you, and who will end up by making you unhappy?

B.-H.L.: Proust has the answer — *again!* He says that you're in love "in your mind," not with "the object." And the great mistake people make is in investing the person one loves with what actually exists only within the person who does the loving.

F.G.: That's from *The Fugitive*. The "material" of love is "immaterial," thought can invest it with whatever qualities it likes. Which accounts for all those painful awakenings, the disenchanted lover who finds it impossible to understand the strength of his attachment once he's fallen out of love. "What came over me? What in the world attracted me to her?"

B.-H.L.: Proust gives two examples — the classic one of the "invert" who has "assembled every beauty under the cap of a tram conductor," and the even stranger one of the Baron de Charlus's Germanophilia — whereas the Narrator loathes Germany. Lovers are like countries — or, better, they're like politics. The emotions they inspire are just as absurd, just as little based on logic, as is attraction to a country or to some political opinion.

F.G.: So that it's better to forget trying to understand them.

B.-H.L.: Or, on the contrary, we should make enormous efforts, bring far more sophisticated instruments into play, instruments that can penetrate the darkest areas of a man's psyche.

F.G.: That being said, there are other cases. Fortunately, there are some people with whom the question never arises. You never say, "But what does he see in her?" but, "How well suited they are to each other — what a wonderful couple they make!" Those more pleasant situations are the ones I'd like us to talk about as we conclude.

B.-H.L.: In the end, there are two groups. You can see it with writers.

F.G.: Again . . .

B.-H.L.: Of course. On the one side you have the group — much the smaller group — of those for whom everything goes right. Baudelaire and La Duval, Scott Fitzgerald and Zelda.

F.G.: Goes right? Do you really think that things went right with Scott and Zelda?

B.-H.L.: Yes, in a way. Because picture them together. You can't help thinking: There was one Zelda on the planet and only one; Scott had to fall for her, so he did — which is exactly what the term femme fatale means, by the way: a woman who is destined to be yours.

F.G.: And a woman who, let it also be said, was obviously no great gift.

B.-H.L.: And then, on the other hand, there are all the others, a vast crowd of them, all the writers whose romantic lives biographers are so eager to delve into — usually without much luck. Mallarmé and his wife. Joyce and poor Nora. Verlaine and the bourgeois girl who ended up replacing Rimbaud. Proust, of course, with Agostinelli. So many, many others. As if the unhappy relationship were the rule. You may say that all relationships are unhappy . . . well, they are, more or less. There are actually some cases — the majority of them — where you have the feeling that fate has fallen down on the job.

F.G.: There's also the amazing Zola couple . . .

B.-H.L.: And so many others!

F.G.: Fate would be a comforting way of interpreting it. Destiny. Some higher power. However, I'm afraid that fate has nothing to do with it and that things couldn't have "gone right" for the ones you've mentioned, no matter what — that they were led astray, misguided, by something very personal . . . although I think that Joyce and Nora . . .

B.-H.L.: Joyce's is an interesting case. Because Nora Barnacle was notoriously uneducated, she was completely indifferent to her husband's work, and to literature in general. But she had that name, which fascinated Joyce, she had that docility, which overwhelmed him. Her way of quite happily going along with his craziest notions. And she was almost breathtakingly ordinary, a die-hard conformist. And she ended up — without knowing it — by being the inspiration for Molly Bloom.

F.G.: Conformist! Have you read her letters? She had a very strong personality and a fierce temper, but Joyce drained it all out of her. He sucked her dry. But how does it happen that a woman "inspires" a creator? And should that be considered a privilege or a disaster? One wonders . . .

B.-H.L.: Privilege or disaster for whom?

F.G.: For the woman, of course.

B.-H.L.: Ah . . . it depends. When it's Zelda, it's a disaster. When it's someone like Gala Dalí, it's a privilege.

F.G.: Gala Dalí is a special case. Highly intelligent, ruthless, spiteful . . . With all the men in her life — Paul Eluard, Max Ernst and, especially, Dalí — she managed to satisfy both her greed for fame and her greed for money. But can a painter's inspiration be compared to that of a writer? It's a very different thing.

B.-H.L.: Why?

F.G.: A woman who inspires a painter is generally his model. The more passive, docile, immobile she is, the better. Whereas a writer's inspiration — it's hard to say quite what she does. Is it the things she says, the things she writes, as with Nora Barnacle?

B.-H.L.: Or the things she doesn't say, the things she will never write. Most often, a writer's muse doesn't know herself the mysterious channels through which she stimulates his imagination.

F.G.: You're probably right.

B.-H.L.: A writer spies on his model, he steals from her. He often does so against the model's will . . . which means that her situation isn't all that different, in the end, from that of the painter's muse. Even if she isn't passive, she's equally unaware of why she was selected to play her role.

F.G.: Although a woman who has been someone's inspiration is usually quite willing to take credit for it. Indeed, she's often very proud of it.

B.-H.L.: Or jealous, terribly jealous, when another woman takes her place. The "demand" to appear in a novel is very great . . . the competition is savage.

F.G.: Until the day comes — another case in point — when the muse revolts. You mentioned Zelda Fitzgerald — wasn't that what happened in her case?

B.-H.L.: It's the case of the muse who has ceased to inspire, who sets out to preserve whatever she can of her former power by destroying everything, by poisoning the writer's work as you would poison a well. Zelda was Scott's inspiration, and then she did all she could to keep him from writing.

F.G.: Zelda is pathetic because she lost her mind. But what about the muse who doesn't know that Fitzgerald is Fitzgerald or Joyce is Joyce, the muse who regards such men as being merely men who like to write? Nora was a good girl, Zelda was a pain in the neck. But in both cases, and although they were complete opposites, what a life a muse must lead if she isn't sustained by the idea that the man is a genius!

B.-H.L.: I don't agree. Zelda knew that Fitzgerald was Fitzgerald, but then, one day, she had had enough and she decided to strike out for herself. She thought: "He's drained me dry, he's sucked the life out of me, he's taken my flesh and blood, he's created a work of literature — why shouldn't I try my hand at it now, why shouldn't I take back what is mine and make my own book out of it?"

F.G.: Don't you find her reaction understandable?

B.-H.L.: She went through Scott's papers. She discovered the outline of a work in progress in which she saw herself depicted more clearly than ever. She said: "No, out of the question, this is *my* novel! This time, I'll be the one to write it." And she did. It's called *Save Me the Waltz*. The critics savaged her: "Second-rate Fitzgerald!" And that's when she went crazy.

F.G.: She had good reason to.

B.-H.L.: What's interesting in Zelda's case is that she broke the pact.

F.G.: What pact?

B.-H.L.: The pact of immortality. The pact that tells a woman: "You forgo your work, you abandon your own desires — and in exchange I'll make you a character in a great novel. What's more, I'll make you the central character in the true novel, the novel of my life. I'll give you a passport to the future, a visa for eternity." Impossible or not, Gala Dalí went along with that. Zelda rebelled against it. And you have the intermediate example of someone like Elsa Triolet, Aragon's muse, who had it both ways — the inspiration of a great writer, immortalized in his poems, but still managing — one never knows! — to make her own little contribution.

F.G.: Another interesting case is that of Alma Mahler. She never believed in her husband's genius for a second. The only composer she liked was Wagner, she hated Mahler's music. And in cases like that, living with a creative genius can be hell.

B.-H.L.: I must admit, I don't know much about her.

F.G.: It's a textbook case. She'd studied composition, she was undeniably talented. But when they got engaged, Mahler said to her: "I'm the composer. From now on, you've only got one profession: making me happy." That's in a famous letter he wrote to her, filled with declarations of love but also demanding that she give up her own work. She went along with it, accepted what you call the "pact." It was self-mutilation. She became the woman who copied her husband's scores, but she never ever believed in his genius. And because of that, she was unfaithful to him, and he was the one who almost went out of his mind with grief. And, of course, he also managed to turn his grief into music, into great music.

B.-H.L.: You're talking about that long letter that begins with his saying that there are feelings so basic to their relationship that they must be clarified once and for all if they're to be happy together? The one that says that any rivalry between them as composers would become "ridiculous and, in time . . . , degrading"?

F.G.: That's the one. Alma eventually became the mistress of Oskar Kokoschka, the painter, who was also put through the wringer, but even so she was a superb inspiration to him and he never really got over her. However, she never went back to composing. Her life with Mahler had ruined that forever.

B.-H.L.: Fine. That's monstrous, upsetting, whatever you like. But why did Alma go along with it? What did she hope to gain from it?

F.G.: Alma was only a girl when she agreed to Mahler's terms, and he was a world-famous conductor by whom she was terribly impressed. I don't know — she probably thought she could get him to change his mind.

B.-H.L.: Another question: what about *her* talent? Are you so sure that she was really all that talented?

F.G.: There's evidence to support it. There are some first-class lieder. She wasn't just some little girl who was playing around with music, she was a great musician. Indeed, Mahler came to see that himself, later.

B.-H.L.: Because there's also the case of Camille Claudel. It's all very well to lament the tragedy of Camille Claudel, but all the same, she was hardly Rodin, was she?

F.G.: I'll go along with you there, but that's not the question. There was room enough for both of them to have a place in the sun.

B.-H.L.: It's not a question of a "place in the sun."

F.G.: What is it that says that one artist must be stifled so that another can breathe, that one of them must be condemned to despair, to insanity, and that it just happens that this always seems to occur to the detriment of the woman? I don't know of any young men Rodin or Mahler crushed under foot and drove insane, even if their output was of less importance.

B.-H.L.: There are all of George Sand's young men . . . or the young men in Madame de Staël's circle. It couldn't have been a great treat to have been a young writer and in love with either George Sand or Germaine de Staël.

F.G.: The fact is, they devoured them whole — but we're talking about great man-eaters, not women who used men for inspiration and ground them down in the process.

B.-H.L.: Françoise, these things have been going on since the beginning of time . . . and they've got nothing to do with relations between men and women. That would be too simple, too easy. Literary history is replete with artists — and of both sexes — who were ground down by the age in which they lived, Baudelaire, for example. I wrote a novel about Baudelaire, who was the archetypical reviled and mistreated poet, destroyed by his age — by Victor Hugo, among others, who was very much a part of that age. Unfortunately, that's the way things are. And it's a dog-eat-dog world.

F.G.: And of all the dogs the most vicious may be the artists, since theirs is a world in which everyone wants to be the greatest, unique, incomparable.

B.-H.L.: What's unclear in Alma's story is that even as a girl she was dreaming of studios and gardens in which she would bring together "the most remarkable men of her time." Mahler. Kokoschka. And then there were also Klimt, Franz Werfel, and I'm probably leaving some out. So the question is: Given that degree of determination, can we still describe it as a sacrifice, a mutilation — aren't we talking about something more like desire, a vocation, fate? Doesn't Alma's case tend to support the hypothesis of the pact of immortality, and how a woman might benefit from it?

F.G.: I don't see the interest of a pact for immortality. I can see entering into some agreement out of love, out of the conviction that you're dealing with a genius in some field —Jenny and Karl Marx, for example — a man on some exalted level. But the lives such women lead are very often terrible ones — not always, not when they can derive strength from the notion that some great work is being accomplished, but when they doubt that the work is great. That's where Alma deserves our sympathy.

B.-H.L.: Obviously.

F.G.: Indeed, none of the more or less well known couples we've been talking about seems enviable to me, at least not from the viewpoint of the woman who's been sacrificed, even if willingly, on the altar of creation. That's not my notion of a successful couple.

B.-H.L.: Oh, if you want a successful couple . . .

F.G.: But that's what we began by talking about: successful couples.

B.-H.L.: True. But I don't like that term.

F.G.: So let's put it another way. Think of the wonderful sense of harmony between equals you sometimes find with a man and a woman who are happy, who enjoy their lives, who seem to embody a joined, united virility and femininity.

B.-H.L.: Joined, united . . . We're not going to go back to that, are we!

F.G.: Sometimes they are even famous people, artists, for example. Or take Bogart and Bacall, for example, or

John Cassavetes and Gena Rowlands. And there are others that the public doesn't necessarily know about, they don't have to be young. But they make a great impression on those around them. Their shared life together is a work of art. They create a field of force, something radiant, something supreme.

B.-H.L.: Yes, "supreme" — I prefer that word.

F.G.: It may not last a lifetime, but all the same there's the pleasure of being together, the mutual respect, the shared interests, a firmness against the corrosion of the world around them, even if no one can really completely escape from it. It's rare, I agree, but it does exist.

B.-H.L.: Your "successful couple" often has a kind of "We've weathered so many storms, surmounted so many crises, and yet see how we've come through them, admire the way we've weathered it all, how we've held firm . . . an old couple polished down from lying, bound together by a whole network of half admissions, of shameful secrets." That's obviously the less glamorous view.

F.G.: Now you're talking about prizes for longevity, couples that boast their infidelities, their betrayals, their forgotten flings, as though they were war wounds. "See how we've managed to make a go of things!" That's depressing. But still, a successful couple is a very beautiful thing. Come on, you know you agree!

B.-H.L.: Let's say that some people may manage to reconcile the irreconcilable.

F.G.: Right.

B.-H.L.: I don't mean a reconciliation between "feminine" and "masculine" — I really don't believe that that's possible. But rather, let's say, between needs, intrusions, reconciliation of the harsh laws of everyday life with the pleasure principle.

F.G.: As long as you desire, truly desire, each other, you find enough strength to live with the laws of everyday life — or at least to keep from being broken by them.

B.-H.L.: Yesterday I was talking about how to tell the difference between love, seduction, and eroticism. Well, let's admit that a wonderful couple represents a rising above that difference, the surmounting of that inevitability. Let's say that they are two people whose love has not faded, nor their erotic feelings, obviously, nor the demands of seduction.

F.G.: I don't know what you mean by the "demands of seduction."

B.-H.L.: In any love affair there comes a moment of seduction. It's there, whether one has sought it or not, that moment when you pretend, pose, cheat, or delude. There's always that moment, usually a very intense one, where one exerts a superhuman effort to appear different from what one is. You look surprised!

F.G.: No, no; I'm listening.

B.-H.L.: Ever since the snake in the Bible, this has been the standard meaning of "seduction." It's been the seducer's modus operandi: choose your disguise, construct it, and then advance behind the mask it creates, flaunt it, hide yourself beneath it — in short, dazzle in order to escape being seen.

F.G.: "Modus operandi" — that's a bit strong. But all right, I agree: you set out to show your best side.

B.-H.L.: Right. And then there always comes the moment — I wouldn't call it the moment of truth, but that moment when even the best mask, the best disguise, ceases to work. Such moments are usually ordinary, trivial moments. For example, the day when lovers discover that they're both sleepy, or that they have a headache, or that they simply look a little tired after a night of fairly intense lovemaking.

F.G.: There's nothing trivial about being sleepy. Sleep and lovemaking go together.

B.-H.L.: Oh? Well, that's true. But I don't like sleep. The spectacle of sleep.

F.G.: Because the other person has got away from you?

B.-H.L.: I don't know. I don't like the abandon sleep represents.

F.G.: Fine. So . . . trivial moments . . .

B.-H.L.: Yes, that moment in which lovers realize that they have a body that isn't made solely to satisfy amorous desires, to engage in the transports of love. And when that happens, you have two options. Some people, most people, lay their cards on the table: "Right, we were lying, poor fools that we were! Ham actors! We won't be caught like that again, from now on it's everything out in the open, if we're tired, we're tired!" And then there are the other people who do the opposite, who opt for continuing, for refining, the pretense — people who will go to any lengths to try to hang on to some illusion. The mask is eventually removed, of course, but it's a gentle process, very gentle, with a lot of maneuvering, many subtleties, many little games and coquetry — "I know that you know, you know that I know, but both of us are going to go on acting as if we didn't know." That's what I mean by "keeping up the demands of seduction." That, for me, is the definition of your "successful couple."

F.G.: I find your definition a little narrow. But of course you do have to know how to meet the requirements of seduction. I would say that a successful couple represents a common will to succeed. It's the product of great care. It's a creation that needs to be worked on on a daily basis — it's never completed, never perfected, it's very tiring, and it's something that can't be done unilaterally.

B.-H.L.: As soon as there's a question of seduction, it "can't be done unilaterally." But as for calling it "tiring" . . . no. Now I think that word's too narrow. I wouldn't call it tiring.

F.G.: Are you saying it's exhausting?

B.-H.L.: Neither tiring nor exhausting. In my view, the scenario never unfolds without some modicum of grace.

F.G.: Obviously. You mustn't be aware it's happening. But all the same, it implies tension, vigilance. The "successful couple" we're discussing deserve the effort put into it.

B.-H.L.: It mustn't be an effort either. Not an effort . . .

F.G.: Well, success certainly isn't the rule. You and I both know more couples who are failures, or who are shaky, than couples who are successful, but the envy the latter usually inspire surely means that there's something in every man and every woman that aspires to that kind of success.

B.-H.L.: Indeed, most often things go badly. A couple are an inevitability or they are a tragedy. Or they are two souls mingling their sorrow, their emptiness. Sometimes it works, or almost works, and then it's like some kind of blessing, a marvel. It's a physical aberration . . . a miracle. That's all that can be said about it.

F.G.: There's obviously no model . . . no magic formula . . .

B.-H.L.: People in love are solitary, you know. One must never forget that they're solitary. Even if they're solitary people who've acquired the odd habit of being unable to do without each other.

F.G.: So what it comes down to is that love is only a cover for some kind of underlying poverty of spirit, and the couple is a way one can be alone in the company of another person — with occasional brief moments of blessed respite.

Well, we're really ending on a low note. Fortunately, it won't prevent a single person from falling prey to the "eternal stings of desire."

Epilogue

The time has come to part. Impossible to complete the exploration of the ground we set out to cover, the ground where so many others have preceded us, where so many will follow us in the future, trying to grapple with the eternal puzzle: What is a man? What is a woman? What is love? What does it mean to fall out of love? If we have managed to contribute in any way, however meagerly, to piercing this mystery by talking frankly about it, these pages may have some meaning. In any event, thank you for these moments we've spent talking together. I'll always remember them fondly.

F.G.

I too will retain a very pleasant memory of this summer and these conversations. I'm not all that sure that they are

likely to enlighten anyone — or to "pierce" any mysteries.
Life, after all, is an apprenticeship, a perpetual apprenticeship. And both you and I have made it very clear that in
these matters there are really no "lessons" to be learned or
taught. But I've liked pretending that there were, and, in
the final analysis, I like this odd book. Falling in love?
Falling out of love? Those are questions that, without you, I
would never have dared to discuss so freely. Thank you.

B.-H.L.

Index